The Neuroscience of Self-Love

Alexis Fernandez-Preiksa

affirm press

affirm
press

First published by Affirm Press in 2022
Boon Wurrung Country
28 Thistlethwaite Street
South Melbourne VIC 3205
affirmpress.com.au

10 9 8 7 6 5 4 3 2

 A catalogue record for this
book is available from the
National Library of Australia

ISBN: 9781922711441 (hardback)

Cover design by Steph Bishop-Hall © Affirm Press
Typeset in 12/18 pt Minion Pro by Post Pre-press Group, Brisbane
Printed and bound in China by C&C Offset Printing Co., Ltd.

For my four grandparents, who are my greatest example of love. I love you and miss you.

Contents

Disclaimer

This book was written to offer general advice on ways to improve your self-love and to provide broad information on neuroscience topics and is not a replacement for professional help. While implementing the strategies included in this book can be transformative, nothing can replace speaking to a professional and seeking help from your doctor. If you feel you suffer from a mood disorder or you have suffered from any trauma, this book is only intended to serve as a gentle push for you to go and seek help to aid your healing journey.

Introduction

HELLO AND WELCOME TO THIS BOOK AND NEW CHAPTER FOR you! I am so excited to be able to bring to you a book that combines neuroscience and mindset tools that you can easily apply to your life. My aim is to get you to understand what goes on behind a thought, a feeling, an emotion and a behaviour. You can't change what you don't acknowledge, and understanding key structures and functions of how the brain works will help you make changes to your relationship with yourself and help you increase your self-love.

How does neuroscience connect to self-love? Through science, we are understanding the organ of the personality: the brain. Just like a cardiologist assists with heart health, neuroscience and psychology can assist with moods, emotions and character traits, which are intrinsically tied to self-love. You cannot fully understand the brain without the mind, and you cannot understand the mind without the brain. Therefore, the science of the brain is unique in the sense that you constantly have to marry the science of neurochemicals and biology with the science of behaviour and psychology. They are intimately linked and shouldn't be separated. Throughout this book, there will be chapters that focus entirely on neurochemicals and connectivity between the brain regions, and other chapters that focus purely on behavioural interventions that will assist with establishing a healthy balance within your brain.

Before you start this book, I urge you to commit to doing each task or exercise as it is laid out. Reading this book from cover to cover without pausing and implementing these tools is not how I intend the reader's experience to be. As you learn, you do. And as you do, you absorb. If you only read, you will take on board a fraction of this information. Don't fall for the trap of telling yourself you will read it again to do the tasks. Commit now and make this the start of your self-love journey. The excuses end here. So, get a notebook and a pen (or something to type on) and let's begin.

I also don't want you to look at this book as just another self-love book. Look at it as your ticket to get further in every single area of your life because, if you commit to reading it and completing the exercises properly, that is what this book will be. Give me (and yourself) your commitment and time, and I will give you the tools to put into practice to make some major changes in your life.

I set out to break things down into digestible chunks. You will first learn what self-love is and how neuroscience is linked to it. Then you will learn how different things, parts of your upbringing and certain experiences, have led you to become the way you are today. I will then give you tools and hacks to implement in your life and you will see how basic actions can gradually but effectively change how your thoughts are formed and how you experience life.

All the exercises and advice I will give you link back to how you can increase your feelings of self-love by restructuring circuits within the brain and modifying habits you have created. They are all heavily interconnected, and you will see that it takes a holistic approach to achieve true self-love, true self-confidence and true happiness. So go all in and see what unfolds for you over the coming weeks, months and years.

1

What Is Self-Love?

SELF-LOVE HAS MANY DEFINITIONS AND MAY BE INTERPRETED differently by every individual. I see it as accepting yourself whole-heartedly and being happy with the person you are. Self-love is treating yourself with respect, prioritising yourself and focusing on your growth and health because you matter to you.

It is also strongly associated with self-compassion; the ability to be patient and understanding of your challenges, to soothe yourself and be there for yourself when you need to regroup or take a break. It is letting go of having to be perfect because you know that won't change who you are. Who you are is the calm presence that exists behind the chaos that may be going on around you. It is not your achievements, it is not your failures and it certainly is not what people think of you.

Self-love is also something that fluctuates, just like your health. And it is very dependent on the attention you give to it. It is comparable to someone who wants to transform their look by eating a particular diet and training regularly at the gym. You can train all you want and follow a diet to get you to your ideal body; however, if you stop suddenly, then the results will start to fade away. You will be at the mercy of what foods are available and what activity you happen to do and, eventually, you will be back where you started.

But don't let this get you down; working on your self-love becomes easier and easier to do. Just like someone who has transformed their body through eating well and training hard, or someone who has put in the time and effort to get a degree or qualification, this kind of lifestyle is something that gets embedded into you through your daily rituals and routines. Before you know it, it not only becomes part of you but also becomes something that you love, so much so that when you don't do it, you feel like you are going without. What I want you to do is implement these tools that I am going to give you and make self-love a daily habit, working on your mind the way you would your body, and soon it will become a part of you.

Know that self-love is the foundation to a successful life in every area: relationships, career and general happiness. If you love and respect yourself, it becomes only natural to want to treat yourself better, to eat well, to move your body, to improve your relationships and to believe in yourself to go far in your career. I would argue that if you prioritise self-love and a healthy mind, everything else will fall into place. Do this first. Focus on your self-love journey first because once you get this down pat, not only will everything else fall into place, but it will also fall into place faster than you expect. When you truly love and respect yourself, your capabilities change, your resourcefulness increases and you begin to move mountains.

What is promising to know, and essential that you remember, is that a thought is literally a chemical and chemicals can help make physical changes in the brain. These changes will give you a different life, a different way of perceiving things and a different way of thinking altogether. Your journey to self-love should be a multi-pronged approach through your actions, beliefs, routines, experiences, self-talk, external statements, external relationships and self-forgiveness. You can't change one thing and keep treating yourself poorly in other areas and expect your brain and beliefs to change completely. The more you do, the better the results. Even if you only implement half of what is recommended in this book, you will still see some significant changes in your life.

2

Your Future Self Is Your Current Self

MOST OF US ARE REALLY GOOD AT THINKING UP IDEAS FOR OUR future. It's not only easy to think of these things but it is also exciting and it feels good. But when it comes to taking the plunge, to starting AND following through, you choke. Why? Because you put way too much responsibility on your future self. You lump all the hard or unpleasant tasks onto the you of tomorrow. Then tomorrow rolls around and you think, 'WHOA, slow down, I'm not in the mood for that amount of action right now, I'm tired!' This is the trap you fall into. Thinking there is a version of yourself somewhere out there in this world that will be willing to do the ground-work to becoming a self-loving legend, with no protest, no procrastination, just enthusiasm; that they will be keen to do what you are not willing to do today.

Ask yourself this. If you are not willing to action that thing RIGHT NOW, what makes you so sure that your future self will? If you can't demonstrate now that you can change something or if you haven't done so in the past (and stuck to a goal), where is the evidence that the future you will want to? If you don't feel the drive or the motivation now, your tomorrow self probably won't, and the you that will exist in three weeks from today won't either.

As part of this love of procrastinating, humans have a compulsion to look at the future through rose-coloured glasses. We think our motivation will be greater than it is now (hence why we start next week). We think we won't feel as hungry, we think we will be in the zone, we think our energy levels will be through the roof, and we think that our confidence will arise out of thin air so we can go and kick ass at work. I'm not saying these things are not possible. You decide what is possible. But to make these decisions for your future self without taking a drop of action now is setting yourself up for disappointment.

Your future self is your current self. The actions you take now and the thoughts you have now determine who you will be in a week, a month and a year down the track. It is the shit you action NOW that determines your future self, not what your future self will do, because that person will never exist if you don't bring them into reality today. Look at who you are now. You are a result of the past you, your actions or inactions, the goals you achieved, the things you procrastinated on and never did, the thoughts you had about yourself.

I am telling you now, your brain will avoid discomfort at any turn; it is a protective mechanism, so let's not get mad at the brain for making procrastination feel like a good idea (more on the science of this later) and just expect that from yourself. If you are resisting something now, why do you think you won't resist it tomorrow? Stop thinking of your tomorrow self as someone different to the you of today. This is why we procrastinate. Firstly, to avoid discomfort, and secondly because we think it will be easier for our future self to do it. And despite it never working for us, literally ever, we still choose to believe that delusion.

If you want to take action tomorrow, then take some action today. If you want to procrastinate tomorrow, procrastinate today.

The way we feel towards ourselves is also heavily based around how we value our time and how much we are willing to do for ourselves. Once you learn the magic of doing your future self a favour, and how good that feels, you will understand that doing something towards your personal growth each day is one of the keys to self-love, happiness and feeling good about yourself and your future.

3

The Pillars of Happiness

I BELIEVE THAT THERE ARE THREE PILLARS WHEN IT COMES TO achieving happiness and self-love. Happiness and self-love go hand in hand, so it is vital that, in order to work on your self-love, you also want to work on your overall happiness. Let's go over my three pillars and then see if you are doing something each day to work towards them.

1. Connection – with others and with yourself
2. Growth – always be working towards something and seeing progress
3. Purpose – feel that you have a strong 'why' and you are working towards that 'why' in some capacity most days.

If you are working on each of these pillars and have a clear understanding of the progress you are making, not only will you start to feel happier overall, but you will also feel happier within yourself. Let's break them down.

Connection

We, as humans, are wired for connection. We literally need it to survive. It provides us with a community, a family and warmth. If you look at humans from a survival perspective, we needed to connect to survive. One of the worst forms of torture is solitary confinement – the removal of human connection. If we don't get it, we risk losing our minds. When we get it and when it is genuine, we feel recharged, we feel energised and heard, we feel part of something greater and we feel loved.

Growth

Humans are ever-evolving beings. We feel this ourselves. If we keep doing the same thing and never change, we see the world pass us by. It is our nature to evolve and we have many evolutions throughout our lifetime. As we experience new things, learn new things and become more resilient, we shed our old skin and come into our new one. We have an instinctive need to grow and this taps into our need for adventure. Your idea of adventure doesn't have to be the same as someone else's. It doesn't have to be skydiving or moving to a different city; it could be joining a chess club and challenging yourself each week. Adventure is in the eye of the beholder, but we all need it to feel fulfilled.

Purpose

When you have a reason for doing something or for existing, it drives you towards something. You literally feel pulled. You know it is a purpose because the more you do it, the more you want to do it. I have had many jobs in my life that I loved, but I definitely did not want to do more of them and I certainly did not want to do them for years to come. I knew they were temporary. However, every time I got feedback from listeners of my podcast telling me that they had been able to implement change with what I taught them, I would feel a surge of energy and also a feeling of warmth. For me, it is the same feeling I get when I make a stranger smile. I probably feel happier than they do in that moment. Your purpose doesn't have to be your life's work and it doesn't have to take hours each day. It could be as simple as, 'I want to make at least three people forget about their troubles each day, if only for a moment'. Something so simple can have an impact. If you work towards your purpose, be it big or small, you will feel like you are always being pulled in the right direction and it won't feel like a struggle. You will feel grounded, calm, happy and excited.

If you feel you have not yet found your purpose, give yourself a challenge this week and come up with one idea that you can do every day for seven days. When you wake up each morning, remind yourself of that purpose and start your day with that intention in mind. Your purpose should involve others (be it other people, animals or nature) and you should aim to feel a connection. When you link purpose with connection, it becomes a positive, never-ending cycle. The more connected you feel, the more you want to give. The more you give to your purpose and to others, the better you feel inside. This is where you feel worthy, validated and loved, because you created it and you are feeling it from the inside. None of it is external, none of it is superficial. There are chapters in this book that explain neurotransmitter release and what these neurochemicals cause you to feel, and how to increase levels of these chemicals. When you get to those chapters, pay close attention to dopamine and serotonin and notice how actions and behaviours that promote connection also promote a healthy release of these feel-good neurochemicals.

4

The Brain's Early Development

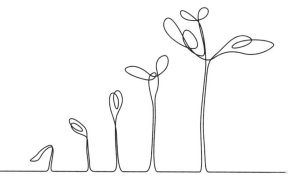

I THINK IT IS IMPORTANT TO GET SOME INSIGHT INTO HOW YOUR brain was wired in your formative first few years of life. Everyone has a way of seeing the world and belief systems around it. You have an idea, a sort of concept, of your surroundings. If the world is a good place to be in or not, whether people (in general) are kind or unkind, if you can rely on others or not, and if you are lovable or not. And you also have a belief system based around yourself and your own abilities, resilience and intelligence. All this is called your internal working model. This is formed very early on in your life according to something called attachment theory – a theory developed jointly by Mary Ainsworth and John Bowlby. It can also be altered later on, for better or for worse, through either a traumatic or impactful time in your life, for example, an abusive relationship, through PTSD or through doing work on yourself and learning how to change this internal working model. For some, this can be done alone, for others it is better done with the guidance of a therapist.

This internal working model can be changed through acknowledgment and consistent work. I think it is always helpful to look back so you can understand why you may think the way you do, but it's also important that you don't keep your focus on the past. And I certainly don't recommend putting blame on others or on your parents. Parents, in general, will raise children how they know best or based on their own internal working model. Blaming parents will likely get you nowhere and will probably keep you in a place of resentment or sadness. This activity of looking back into your past serves purely to make sense of why you think or behave the way you do, why your brain has been wired this way and how that can be turned around. It is simply to help you understand yourself better, not to have you living in your past.

Let's begin with attachment theory

Attachment theory explains how your first few years of life can shape how you perceive relationships with others, the world and yourself in your future. These formative years – and possibly any impactful event – can actually shape your brain's circuitry in a particular way, so you may perceive a neutral stimulus as a stress or as something of no importance. As you have probably guessed by now, your attachment style can have a big impact on how you view yourself and your abilities. By understanding this and acknowledging your particular attachment style, you can learn to be less reactive to situations and become more observational of your feelings and emotions, things that happen to you or how people treat you. Attachment theory will impact your levels of self-love because it has formed the foundations of how you perceive yourself. I recommend identifying what your attachment style is to learn about where you are starting from and where you want to go.

From when a child is born until the first few years of age, the brain is going wild forming a whole array of new connections between neurons and between brain regions. As these connections form, the child begins to form a relationship with the world around them and they begin to gain an understanding of security and relationships, initially with their primary caregivers – in most cases, their parents.

It is during this time that a belief system is created and a blueprint is formed in their mind. What a relationship should look like, what trust looks like, what failure looks like, how the world will treat them, if the world is a kind place, if they will be supported or not, and also what they think of themselves and their own abilities. If these beliefs are never questioned, then they will act on them and find relationships that feed into this thought pattern and justify situations that fit this blueprint. Only when you can identify these patterns can you decide if you want and are willing to change them. Without acknowledgement, it is almost impossible to make a change.

5

The Four Attachment Styles

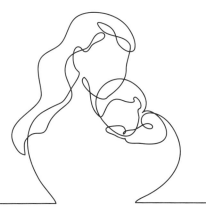

NOW I'M GOING TO BREAK DOWN THE FOUR MAIN ATTACHMENT styles and show you what the internal working model is for each style.

Secure attachment

55–65% of the population

In secure attachment the child learns that they are always supported and can always rely on their caregiver. Because they always have this secure base, they start to gain confidence within themselves and start to explore. The parent allows for this exploration but is always there for the child when they return. This makes the child feel that it is safe to explore, so the next time they go further and further, gaining more and more independence while always feeling loved and supported. This doesn't mean that the parent never slips up or makes a mistake, or that they are there for the child one hundred per cent of the time; no one is perfect or that consistent. But, in a secure upbringing, the parent is able to repair situations well. If the parent couldn't support the child when they were scared or sad, they then would do it the moment they were able to. They explain things to the child and keep an open line of communication. If repair happens after any problem, then the child still feels a sense of security and safety.

Their internal working model is that they are safe, they are loved, the world is generally a safe and kind place, and that they are fine. Through this stable and consistent interaction they learn to soothe themselves when they are scared or anxious and learn to become independent. When they grow up and start to form new relationships, they know that they can depend on someone, but also, if the relationship is not a healthy one, they feel that they can walk away because they feel worthy and okay being without a partner. They are okay being alone and independent because they don't find their self-worth in a partner.

There is consistency with the parenting. If the child is in pain, they are comforted. If they do something good, they get a positive response. If they do something bad, there are repercussions that are proportionate to what they have done.

Almost all of their future relationships, and the way they interact with others, including strangers, are based around this secure attachment.

Internal working model

I am loved. I am worth it. I can depend on people.
The world is a good place. I am capable.

Insecure avoidant attachment

20–30% of the population

In insecure avoidant attachment there are inconsistencies with what the child can expect from the parent, who is not in tune with what the child wants. This is normally based on how the parent was parented and they, in turn, model what they know. One day the parent might be fine with the child doing something, the next day they punish the child for the same action. They let the child cry it out often, so the child begins to feel that when they need someone, they are not there in that moment. The child doesn't know if they will be supported when they need it. Or the support is inconsistent enough that they can't rely on it, so they need to take things into their own hands. A lot of rebellious behaviour at school can stem from this pattern.

They are cared for and there is affection and love, but there is an inconsistency in the communication between parent and child. So if the child gets in trouble, the parent shuts them down instead of talking about it and discussing what happened and what would have been a better outcome. This inconsistency is common in parents who have a very old-school style of parenting and have this idea that children should be seen and not heard. Or that they shouldn't have to apologise to their child if they were in the wrong. The child does not feel heard and gets frustrated.

Someone with insecure avoidant attachment will base their future relationships on this model. They enter relationships thinking, 'I've been let down, so you need to earn my trust. I don't know if you will be there for me when I need it so I will push you away and test you'. They often hold the idea that everyone gets f*cked over in relationships, and that trust is easily broken and hard to regain so they must take things into their own hands.

Externalised behaviours, such as rebelliousness or anger, are common and the person can't be settled as easily as those with a secure attachment internal working model. This behaviour is nothing too serious, and mainly manifests in rebelling in the classroom. They rebel because they feel disrespected or not heard so they mirror that treatment.

Internal working model

I am loved but I don't know if I can depend on people.
The world may be a good place but I am
scared to be let down. I am capable but may not
be able to rely on others for help, so I won't.

Insecure ambivalent attachment

10–15% of the population

In insecure ambivalent attachment the parent is responsive but inconsistent. They can be close and warm, but can also be intrusive and over-attentive – this is also referred to as 'helicopter parenting'. They keep interrupting what the child is doing and telling them how to do it or that they are doing it wrong. They help them too much and don't allow the child to make their own errors and learn from them. The child doesn't get much freedom because the parent is always overseeing what they do. They always finish their child's sentences and are too eager to help them do physical tasks without giving the child the opportunity to work it out for themselves. The child wants the parent to be there for them, but not in their face all the time. The parent is overprotective and this becomes unsatisfying for both the child and parent.

Feelings flip between empathy and frustration, guilt and blame. The relationship is close and very loving but also intense, so the child gets frustrated. Often, when the parent is too busy, the child demands attention because they are used to it, but when they don't get the attention they become frustrated and confused and need reassurance constantly. They don't feel confident in their abilities because they haven't been given the freedom to make mistakes and know it will be okay. So they then ask the same question several times; they learn that the more fuss they make, the more attention they get. If they ever want attention, instead of asking for it, they make a huge fuss, the parent loses their temper and then the child gets sad and the parent feels guilty.

Everyone is missing the throw and catch of communication. When the child wants the attention, it's not there, and when they don't want it, it is there in an overbearing way. It's not damaging to the child because they are loved and cared for, and they do feel safe, but they become very needy. They need constant reassurance. And the more attention they get when they are being needy only reaffirms that their

THE FOUR ATTACHMENT STYLES

insecure behaviour is the right thing to do. They don't feel abandoned or alone, they just feel insecure and unable to regulate their own emotions because they don't know how to soothe themselves.

The child fears expressing true emotions. They are worried the caregiver won't be there for them when they have opened up in that crucial moment, so they are not comfortable opening up and expressing true emotions. They would rather cry and make a fuss instead.

In future relationships they can become very clingy or insecure and needy, and are always seeking reassurance and constantly checking up on their partner. They need to be able to access and communicate with their partner at all times. Their internal dialogue is, 'I am scared that you may leave me, so I'm going to cling to you even more'. When they are broken up with, it is like a self-fulfilling prophecy. They saw it coming.

Internal working model

I am lovable but I am fearful of being alone and scared of being broken up with. People must earn my trust. I am capable but not independent. I need reassurance constantly to know that I won't be abandoned and to prove that I am capable.

Disorganised (fearful) attachment

10–20% of the population

Disorganised attachment often occurs in situations where the child has been abandoned or abused, but not in all cases. The child has no consistency, and additionally feels either neglected or abused. They may interpret the most toxic of behaviours as a representation of love, because that is all they have experienced from their primary caregivers. Therefore, they may accept a lot of awful behaviour in relationships later in life, as they believe it to be love.

These children don't have a strategy to manage their emotions. They never saw a consistent model so they struggle to know what works for them. They don't specifically engage in avoidance behaviours, and they don't over-dramatise. They don't know what to expect from others, and because of this they don't know how to settle themselves. They don't have a consistent pattern of behaviour. The child either sees that their own parent is frightened or is frightening. For example, they may see their parent or caregiver being aggressive towards them or see their parents being aggressive towards each other, without ever seeing a resolution. They don't know what to do in this situation; they want to help but are pushed away, so it is very confronting, confusing and scary for them.

Fright without a solution or repair will lead to disorganised attachment. If this continues throughout childhood, it will carry on into adulthood. Disorganised attachment is more common with children whose parents have experienced loss, trauma or addiction. The child is then more susceptible to mental health conditions, addictive behaviours, anxiety, attention disorders, chronic stress and a lower IQ because they are not developing at the rate of their peers. They struggle to retain what they have learnt and this may cause them to fall behind their peers, which then can cause them to lose interest at school.

As adults they are more likely to accept abusive relationships in their life. They see this as love and think, 'That's just how they show their love'. Their model of what a relationship is was engrained in them as a child, so they think that it is normal to have a very volatile relationship, and that a lot of anger and passion must mean love.

Internal working model

The world is generally not a safe place. I can't rely or depend on anyone as I will probably be let down. People cannot be trusted. I doubt my own abilities. I am not lovable.

EXERCISE

Pause now and have a look at your own situation, and answer the following questions:

- How do I react to things?
- What do I think my internal working model is?
- Do I think the world is generally a good place?
- Do I think people are generally kind to me?
- Am I lovable? Am I loved?
- Am I capable of achieving things?

This will give you some insight into what attachment style you may have.

6

Synaptic Pruning in the Early Days

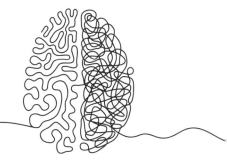

WHILE YOUR ATTACHMENT STYLE IS BEING FORMED IN THE first few years of life, your brain is going through huge changes. The number of synapses (connections between neurons) is rapidly increasing. The brain is taking in a huge amount of information and learning how to process it, so its first job is to go wild, making as many synapses as may be necessary later on. The brain is starting to form a kind of scaffolding on which things will be built or strengthened later on.

From the age of two to three until around ten, the brain then goes through a process called pruning. This pruning hits a second wave in adolescence, but can still occur at much lower rates into adulthood. In the initial pruning phase in childhood, the brain prunes out and eliminates around fifty per cent of the extra synapses that it deems unnecessary. How does it determine if it is not necessary? It depends on how much it is being used; if you don't use it, you lose it. This happens in order for the brain to become more efficient. There is no point supplying energy to pathways that are not needed, so the brain will get rid of them. A number of disorders are linked to abnormalities in the pruning process. Autism spectrum disorder and epilepsy are shown to be linked to 'under pruning'. If there is a lack of pruning and too many synapses, then there may be an overload of activity instead of a focused brain response. You can see how important the process is.

The pathways that are used more get strengthened. Cells that fire together wire together. This wiring makes for a more efficient brain. Your brain thinks, 'Well if I am always in fear, then I'm going to put more effort and attention into these pathways and networks so I can access them and my reactions to fear more easily' (for example, actions of flight or fight). The same goes for when the brain learns a skill such as walking, playing tennis or driving a car. Initially it is difficult, takes up all of your conscious attention and even feels clumsy, but as those networks get strengthened, the skill, movement or thought becomes swifter, automatic and efficient. The brain learns, through repetition, where to strengthen pathways. If you have a strengthened pathway of a behaviour that you don't like, it's not because your brain is being an asshole, it is because that behaviour has been repeated enough that your brain then makes the process more efficient for you. Your brain is trying to do you a favour.

How connectivity between brain regions occurs with different styles of attachment

Secure attachment

There is more development through the prefrontal cortex, which is involved in executive thinking, being socially aware, and understanding communication and consequences, so there is strong connectivity between the brain regions.

Everyone develops emotion and fear processing; however, those with a secure attachment have a good connectivity between their fear circuit and prefrontal cortex. Due to this strong connectivity, the reasoning centre can communicate to the emotion- or fear-processing centre (amygdala) and tell you to relax or calm down, and this can be done pretty quickly.

Insecure avoidant or insecure ambivalent attachment

This connectivity is okay but not as great as for someone with a secure attachment style. This person is more likely to get stuck in the anxiety or fear loop, and their ability to soothe themselves is not as strong. Therefore, they are less likely to put themselves in a vulnerable position as they will want to avoid pain or abandonment.

Disorganised attachment

This connectivity is even more affected. There is a lot of confusion and it makes it very difficult to use reasoning to change a long-held belief. The person's internal working model is very negative. The fear circuitry is stronger and more dominant so the defensive walls are up as they feel they cannot trust people, and their prefrontal cortex is less dominant over these emotions.

The less connectivity between the prefrontal cortex and the amygdala, the more your fear circuitry will have power over you. You may even start to interpret or perceive a neutral response as being a threat, which is often the case in disorganised attachment. You may notice someone with a neutral facial expression or read a neutral comment or text message and interpret it as a threat or an attack, and then you may go down the fight or flight path, getting defensive over something that had no meaning behind it. This is all down to how your brain has been wired to interpret things. The more active your amygdala is, the greater chance you have of having an anxiety disorder, depression, chronic stress or attention disorders. In these situations, it is harder to calm down and harder to reason with this stress response.

7

Your Thoughts Create Your Reality, Literally

NOW YOU CAN SEE THAT YOUR THOUGHTS DIRECT YOUR perceptions and interpretations, and how you come to conclusions. These then become beliefs and they directly impact your life experience from moment to moment, day to day. In this chapter we will look at ways that our thoughts can totally distort our perception and, therefore, what we feel and experience.

Let's start with 'toxic positivity', because that is not what I am advocating for here. There is a big difference between that and taking on new thoughts and statements that are actually helpful. I am not about 'Just think happy thoughts and everything will be fine'. I can't stand that. What is toxic positivity? That idea that you can say 'Everything is FINE' and 'Just be happy. Stop being negative. Why don't you just try to be positive?' and all of a sudden everything will miraculously be fine. I personally find this talk out of touch and it does not consider people's personal situations and the way they have been wired to perceive and react to situations. It's all well and good for someone who has grown up feeling loved and safe, with everything at their disposal, who has never suffered from a mood disorder or excessive stress, or who isn't currently going through something intense to say these things, but I think that kind of 'positivity' is, for most people, more frustrating than it is helpful. Affirmations DO work, but you must believe what you are saying and, if what you are saying feels too far removed from your reality or what you believe to be possible for you, then no matter how much you repeat it, it will never make you feel better.

I think it runs deeper than just saying a positive statement. You can't just automatically start to feel happy and carefree when you have been wired differently and when your belief systems don't support these new ideas. Now that you understand attachment theory and how your internal working model works, it will begin to make sense why your brain will jump to conclusions regarding any new situation. This is your subconscious mind trying to save you time. It is telling you that, based on the past, I predict the future will be like this, so I will react accordingly. The brain likes to save time, be efficient and, most importantly, protect you. It may feel like your brain is your enemy, but it's really just trying to help you based on what it knows. However, if you don't acknowledge and then intercept these thoughts, you will never be or think any different to your past. With enough conscious effort, you can rewrite and rewire your brain to automatically turn to new and helpful beliefs. Eventually you will have the ability to change your internal working model.

First, you need to find a statement that you can resonate with, that you can FEEL. Something that triggers a visceral response. Your body is intuitive and you know in an instant if you are telling yourself a lie or the truth. The moment you recognise something as a flat out lie, you won't accept it. So let's look into the mechanisms behind what we believe to be true and why.

Confirmation bias

It begins with what you have been taught without questioning or what you have experienced firsthand. Once you believe something strongly enough, then your **reticular activating system** (see below) will kick in and your thought habits will lean towards a confirmation bias, which almost everyone does to some degree. You start to only notice or actively seek out thoughts that confirm what you believe in and then either not notice, block out or dismiss the pieces of information that counter what your belief is. You rule it out as an outlier, a one-off or a blatant lie. You can see this happening around you all the time especially in this information age where so many people have internet access. People will form a belief, strengthen it and then only seek out information that backs up their belief, while ignoring, dismissing or attempting to dismantle any counterargument.

The reticular activating system (RAS)

This part of the brain is like a filter. It helps with selective attention and filtering out unnecessary information, and highlights the relevant information that may be of use to you. You are constantly flooded with all kinds of information each day and it would be impossible for you to place your conscious attention on all these things. It is endless and if you didn't filter it out it would be completely overwhelming.

The RAS uses what you have either liked, or had an emotional reaction to at some point, to determine what will be filtered in. It bases its actions on your past. So if you are about to purchase a red car, you see red cars everywhere. If you are always thinking people are out to get you, you find clues or hints or examples of dodgy people way more than someone who thinks everyone is kind and helpful. You subconsciously seek out what you already believe to be true. And you filter out what you don't. The RAS doesn't do this to make you biased, but instead to save you time on stimulus that may not be relevant at all.

This is not a bad thing, because you can train your RAS to start to seek out the things you now want in your mind: thoughts, beliefs and concepts, as well as corresponding experiences and encounters with people. This book will give you a whole bunch of hacks to put into place, and the more you do them, the more your RAS will seek out things that confirm this new lifestyle, seeking out people and opportunities that align with it as well. Use this to your advantage. And if, right now, you are always noticing the negative or the bad in people, understand that is what you have primed your RAS to do and it can be changed simply by shifting what you put most of your focus on. It won't happen overnight but the shift will happen as you start to implement the hacks that you learn in this book.

Search for truths in your mind

When it comes to science, a good scientist is one who is always in search of the truth. They should be able to gladly accept if someone can prove them wrong in something (if there is sufficient evidence to back it), as it will get them closer to the truth. The ideal is that they strive to work alongside others, challenging each other and themselves to get as close to the truth as possible. If we did this within our communities, we would be better communicators and we wouldn't be as quick to judge or as quick to shut someone down who disagrees with us. Most people don't do this, and a lot of people like to ignore evidence and end up feeling attacked or becoming aggressive and defensive, pushing people further away from each other. We see this in society and on social media all the time; arguments and not debates.

Notice how this can affect the relationship you have with yourself? If you don't try to find counter evidence to the limiting beliefs you have created for yourself, then you will never expand further from where you are today. In order to grow, to love yourself more, you need to start to change your thoughts FOR REAL and not just by saying a positive affirmation here or there. You need to be in search of the truth. You need to find the middle ground, to be able to remove emotional attachment to statements or old beliefs and see them for what they are.

What does this look like? You have to be willing to look at something from an opposing view. It's like you are on a debating team. You can stand there and argue all you want but there will ALWAYS be counter evidence or opinions that are opposite to those views. I want you to play the role of the debater to your own thoughts.

It is simple. Say one of your typical thoughts in your mind is, for example, 'I always struggle to focus, that's why I can't study', then think of a counterargument like, 'I can find something to pique my interest and gain tools to help improve my focus. I know other people who have done this/I can think of some examples where that is the case'. Or, for example, 'I can't do that because my body won't allow me' and then counter it with, 'My body is capable of learning things. Here is a list of things I have trained my body to do ...'

You are playing the role of the debater. And if you find this to be too confronting, then get someone you trust, and can be open and vulnerable with, to play that role. For each statement you give about a belief you hold about yourself, there will be a counterargument.

EXERCISE

Write down the top three strongest negative statements that you tell yourself.

Next to each, write three opposing statements to put the negative statements into perspective.

In future, each time you find yourself starting to use one of these negative statements, immediately counter it with the opposing statement you came up with. It gets easier with time, trust me.

8

Validation, Self-Worth and Confidence

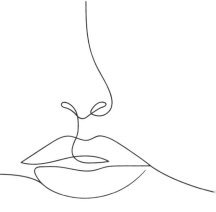

THE NEUROSCIENCE OF SELF-LOVE

CONFIDENCE AND SELF-VALIDATION ARE VERY DEEP INSIDE you and have nothing to do with other people. Confidence does not mean being the loudest in the room, the first person to speak, the one to make a decision first or the funniest in the group. Instead, it is feeling comfortable in your own skin, regardless of where you are or who you are around. It is the ability to be the same person around your crush as you are with your best friend. It's the inner peace you feel when you accept yourself and you don't give that responsibility to those around you. The loud unconscious mind may lead you to believe that it is up to others to determine your worthiness, but this is only the case because you haven't put a stop to it.

I once asked a whole bunch of my podcast listeners what they wish they didn't need from others. They all answered anonymously and couldn't see each other's answers, and out of thousands of answers the overwhelmingly popular response was 'validation'. Almost everyone wished they didn't need to feel validated by others and wished they could just feel it for themselves.

So what can we do about it? What does 'validate' mean? It means to demonstrate or support the truth or value of something OR to prove the accuracy.

When you seek validation, you are asking that person to prove your value, your worth. And when you do that, you affirm that you are not capable of doing it for yourself.

You enter this continuous cycle of seeking it from others, feeling relief when you get it, then getting hooked on that temporary feeling after a while you forget how to do it for yourself.

Where do you seek validation?

You innately seek validation from others. That's normal and it is not a terrible thing if you look at it from a survival perspective – we are wired to need to be part of a community, to be accepted by our group. Our relationship with our community determines our survival. If you go way back, if you didn't fit in with your tribe, you were cast out of the community and you didn't survive. Naturally, we want others to like us, we want others to tell us we are doing the right thing, so we feel safe. When we are liked or complimented, we get a surge of feel-good neurotransmitters, such as oxytocin, dopamine and serotonin. We feel good when this happens, so we want to do it again, creating a positive feedback loop.

The main way of seeking validation is by trying to be the best, the prettiest, the most confident or the smartest, or by being right. We think that this is what gives us value. We see it around us in culture and movies so we naturally try to mirror this image of success or near-perfection.

But should we be placing all our sense of validation in the hands of those around us? Can we shift where we seek approval from to make it come from within, or is it a biological need to get it from others? The answer is both, but most of your validation should come from within because if you only seek it from others, you fall at the mercy of their opinions or the mood they may be in at the time.

When should you seek validation from others?

When you are doing something that directly impacts others (your partner, friends or community) then it is beneficial for you to get feedback on your actions or your behaviour. This is healthy and helps improve your relationships. If you did whatever you wanted and didn't give a flying f*ck how that impacted others, and had no concern for those around you, you probably would have no friends, and rightly so. Relationships are a two-way street and we need to respect that.

Additionally, you may seek validation or approval from people professionally. These are your mentors or superiors and, at times, you want your work validated by people who can help you grow or improve. Just make sure you are sticking to the people that are relevant, such as those directly connected to your work, who know what they are talking about.

When shouldn't you seek validation from others?

Pretty much in every other scenario; in situations that only directly impact you, such as what you choose to do for a career, where you live, how you spend your money as an individual, or what you wear. Everyone has their own opinion of what they think is appropriate, what is right or wrong, pretty or ugly, smart or not. What may be a brilliant idea for some is ridiculous and irresponsible for others. A great outfit for one is a nightmare for someone else. Your choices for what you do with your life – your career, your style, your hobbies – are all subjective. So, it would be impossible to get everyone to validate you as some would love what you do and others would not. Your only solution would be to be super bland so as not to incite a reaction from others. But then you end up making yourself small and only hindering yourself.

If you get others to validate your personal life decisions and that is where you get your self-esteem from, the moment someone doesn't like what you do, you feel hurt. The moment you get a 'bad review' you think about it for ten times longer than a good review. You could have one hundred people say something to make you feel validated and then ONE person says something negative and it ruins your day. It's not worth it. The scales are not even and the feeling after a positive response versus a negative one is not proportionate.

Stop putting people on a pedestal, they won't like you more

If you do something purely to gain the acceptance of someone else, it reeks of desperation (unfortunately). Here you are, putting someone on a pedestal, going out of your way to make them like you, and your actions backfire. Instead of them thinking, 'Wow, this person is so kind and generous. We agree on everything. I want them in my life every day', they are thinking, 'This person is nice ... but not authentic' or 'This feels forced'. They won't think twice about the encounter. It leaves you feeling rejected or fighting for more. The moment you put someone (a crush or someone in a social circle) on a pedestal, your authenticity goes out the window.

Why do I put on an act for people to like me? Why do I struggle to be authentic?

Being authentic is one of the greatest forms of self-love. You are telling yourself and everyone else, 'I am happy this way and I don't need to pretend to be someone else in the hope that you will like me more. And if you don't like certain things about me, I am okay with that; that is your opinion, not mine'. It is a huge statement and when you feel that way people sense this energy and gravitate towards it. People like people who are comfortable in their own skin, not someone who tells them what they want to hear, who agrees with everything and who bows down to them. Yet so often people put on a show to be liked because they think their authentic self will not be enough.

And we put on an act to feel protected – it is your protective blanket so if you get rejected you can still say to yourself, 'Oh I wasn't being me, they didn't get the chance to see the real me'. You feel protected and so you do it more. Because the thought of them rejecting the real you would be terrifying, especially if we are talking about a romantic interest. However, this protective blanket is doing you more harm than good. It is delaying the inevitable, that a wrong match will always be a wrong match.

You need to rip that bandaid off faster. It is one thousand times better to be turned down by someone early in a relationship because you are not the right match instead of wasting time holding onto hope while not being your true self. And all this time-wasting makes you fall harder for someone and take longer to recover.

If someone doesn't like the real you, they are not bad or stupid for not seeing it or not trying, they are just not for you. Remove the pressure from yourself and others. The sooner you can think this way with less attachment to the outcome, the less time you spend mourning a relationship that has not even begun. Liberate yourself. Being your true self helps weed out the people you would never click with in the first place.

If you want to feel worthy, start by giving value to others, without expecting anything in return. Expectation is what kills happiness. Help someone, help an animal or the environment, share or give something. Give value however you want, but do it for the process, not for external validation. If you want to feel more value, give more value. You will never get it by looking for it because it can only ever be felt and found within. To put your sense of worth in other people's opinions or compliments is you giving your power away.

9

Everything Psychological Is Biological

THIS NEXT SECTION WILL GO THROUGH AN ARRAY OF different neuromodulators, also known as neurochemicals, neurotransmitters or hormones. Many of the actions we take play a role in the release cycle of certain chemicals, which then influence our emotions, mood, learning, memory, sleep and how we interpret rewards. Not only are neurochemicals vital for every process that occurs between neurons, but they are also instrumental in creating our feelings, emotions and overall mood. For a long time, behavioural psychology and neuroscience were two separate fields, but as science in both areas has evolved, the two schools of thought have been able to come closer and closer together. Behaviour is what we see; it is the result (or the symptom) of what is occurring at a biological and chemical level within the brain. But understanding the workings of the brain and how chemicals act has not been easy. You cannot just open someone's brain up and observe a thought or the actions of a neurotransmitter. And without psychology and the ability to understand mood disorders, emotions and even physical responses to stimuli, our grasp of the brain's functions would be limited. The brain is unique in the sense that it is the house of the personality, and what occurs in the brain directly impacts your personality. You can scan someone's shoulder and see what is wrong, go in and fix it, and it would likely be fixed and have zero impact on that person's personality. As we can't do that to the brain, psychology and neuroscience need to be very closely linked to grasp the full picture of what is going on.

While not fully understood, mood disorders are an imbalance of these chemicals or an irregular release of them. Antidepressants and other chemical modulators are designed to regulate the availability of these neurochemicals between neurons where connections are made. However, this is not the only option for altering the availability of certain neurotransmitters within your brain. In addition to taking medication to treat mood disorders, there are many lifestyle changes you can incorporate into your day, physically and psychologically, to achieve a healthier balance of these chemicals within your brain.

Everything you do is the cause of a chemical-driven communication between neurons. The same goes for every thought you have. And if you understand that cells that fire together wire together, you will understand that the more often a particular thought is made the stronger that wiring in the brain will be. These chemicals control these connections, and the frequency at which you think of these thoughts or perform certain behaviours will determine the strength of that connection – repetition equals strong pathways. You will see that some behaviours and thoughts (and even self-talk) will encourage higher levels of neurochemicals that forge destructive networks within the brain. The kind that leads to overthinking, catastrophising, anxiety and even poor focus and lack of sleep. Other behaviours will encourage the release and production of chemicals in the brain that will be protective and improve your health and overall happiness and wellbeing.

The following chapters will give an overview of a few of the main neurochemicals and proteins associated with mood (although not all, as there are too many chemicals involved to explain all of them here). I will explain what you can do to regulate or increase the presence of them and how they affect your mood and behaviour.

10

Serotonin and Tryptophan

SEROTONIN IS COMMONLY KNOWN AS THE FEEL-GOOD OR happiness neurotransmitter. It acts as a natural mood stabiliser and is derived from the essential amino acid tryptophan. To better understand how serotonin is made available in the brain I need to also talk about tryptophan. I'm going to break it down without getting too deep or too complicated. I'll be giving you a bit of an insight, but keep in mind that there is a whole lot more involved with the process beyond what is written in this chapter. So, let's dive straight in!

Both serotonin and tryptophan play a role in mood stabi-lising and homeostasis (keeping everything stable and balanced) within the brain. Serotonin, like pretty much every neurochemical and hormone, is involved in a lot of things. Most chemicals in the body play many different roles. The body and brain are very efficient and like to assign several tasks to different chemicals or brain regions. This is a blessing but also makes it confusing for scientists to pinpoint ways of increasing, decreasing or harnessing certain chemicals that are either produced within the brain or taken as a medication or supplement.

Serotonin is derived from an essential amino acid called tryptophan that is present in our diet. Basically, essential amino acids cannot be synthesised by the body so they must come from your diet. Tryptophan is a precursor to serotonin but can also be converted into other things. It can go down neurotoxic or neuroprotective pathways, and you will see in a bit how your actions can play a role in determining which pathway tryptophan will go down.

Serotonin does a lot. It is a mood stabiliser, plays a role in memory formation and the feeling of reward, and it helps regulate cortisol (the stress hormone) and growth hormone release. Growth hormone is, of course, important for growing but also helps you age in a healthy way and is involved in muscle repair and speeding up the healing process after an injury. Serotonin is also found in large amounts in the stomach and intestines as it controls bowel movements and function, but serotonin in the brain is what is believed to be linked to mood, and low levels of it (or tryptophan) are linked to mood disorders.

It is involved in sleep regulation and circadian rhythms and, if serotonin levels are low, so is melatonin (a chemical involved with the onset of sleep) because melatonin is synthesised from serotonin. When sleep is poor, it has a negative impact on cognitive function across all domains and influences mood as well. Additionally, when you are sleep deprived, your body tries hard to keep you awake by releasing more cortisol, which then suppresses serotonin, and this then sets off a bit of a vicious cycle of poor sleep and low mood. Low levels of serotonin may also affect your appetite. If serotonin levels are low, there is an increase in anger, a decrease in self-esteem and a decrease in the pain threshold, making you experience more pain. Attention, concentration, emotion and learning are all linked to healthy levels of serotonin and, additionally, this neuro-chemical helps the fight or flight response, allowing you to react at optimal levels when necessary. This is different to chronic stress, which you will read more about in the following chapters.

Low levels of serotonin and tryptophan are associated with depression and other mood disorders; however, it is a lot more complicated than that. There are many more factors that cause depression. Serotonin is known to positively impact and help regulate moods as well. When someone has a healthy balance of serotonin, they are calmer, less volatile and stressed, and have happier moods and increased focus.

This is where it gets a little complex. Tryptophan is broken down and can go down several metabolic pathways. The first is the serotonergic (serotonin-producing) pathway, where it goes through a process of having a hydroxyl group added to the molecule, converting it into serotonin.

Another pathway it can go down is the kynurenine pathway. (There are a whole bunch of things that happen in between but, to spare your brain, I will try my best to keep the details to a minimum.) Whichever hormones or chemicals are present at the time will determine the pathway tryptophan will go down.

If tryptophan goes down the kynurenine pathway, it can get converted into quinolinic acid, which can become neurotoxic due to how it increases excitation in the brain. It works by ramping up the effects of glutamate (a major excitatory neurotransmitter) within the brain. When glutamate levels and excitability are too high, the balance between cells is thrown off and this can have neurotoxic effects, which can lead to cell death (which is obviously a bad thing as it is what reduces brain mass and communication between brain regions, and is partially responsible for neurodegeneration).

Cortisol (the stress hormone) is one of the key players that will cause tryptophan to go down this kynurenine pathway. If there is a lot of inflammation, emotional or physical chronic stress, then tryptophan will likely be converted into quinolinic acid. When this happens, you also get a reduction of available tryptophan that could be converted into serotonin.

Now for some better news. There is an enzyme called kynurenine aminotransferase that stops the conversion of tryptophan into quinolinic acid (that neurotoxic stuff we don't love) and makes kynurenic acid instead. Kynurenic acid does the exact opposite of quinolinic acid and is neuro-protective. Instead of increasing excitability, it decreases it. It turns down the effects of glutamate, thereby protecting the neurons and preventing cell death due to over-excitability. This is great as it can even out the negative or destructive effects of quinolinic acid.

This is where it gets exciting. The enzyme that converts quinolinic acid into kynurenic acid (kynurenine aminotransferase) is activated during moderate to high intensity exercise. The more of it you do, the higher the chances that tryptophan will have positive effects instead of toxic ones. Your behaviour, your actions and habits can literally change what chemicals are being synthesised or blocked, which then influence your mood, sleep and brain health. This goes for both positive and negative actions. On one hand you have exercise, which has neuroprotective effects, and on the other you have chronic stress, which increases chronically higher levels of cortisol release.

Now you can see how each chemical within the body and central nervous system is influenced by other chemicals around it. Things that already exist within your body can act differently and have positive effects just by changing a few behaviours. These chemicals are not acting alone; the body is like a fine-tuned machine where all the moving parts must work together. The great news is that what will help create a good balance for one thing is also going to help in other things. You will see in the coming chapters how exercise plays a very crucial role in regulating these chemicals to reduce anxiety and stress, and to increase focus, creativity and, of course, overall happiness.

11

Brain-Derived Neurotrophic Factor

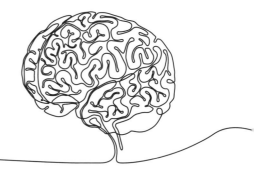

BRAIN-DERIVED NEUROTROPHIC FACTOR (BDNF) IS A PROTEIN that promotes the survival, maintenance and growth of neurons. It is active at the connection site between neurons in an area called the synapse, and this is where cell communication occurs. As humans learn and evolve, these synapses must learn to change and adapt and this process of adaptation is called synaptic plasticity. BDNF is very helpful at regulating this process of plasticity, which is essential for learning, memory and improved connectivity between brain regions. The better your plasticity, the better your recovery from injury or trauma to the brain, and the easier it is to rewire your brain or retrain yourself to do something or think a certain way. Your ability to bounce back or be resilient is increased when BDNF levels are healthy.

In people with mood disorders, such as depression and anxiety, there is a lower amount of BDNF available. Several neurodegenerative diseases, such as Alzheimer's disease and Parkinson's disease, are associated with decreased levels of BDNF. Antidepressants and therapy are some ways to increase the levels of BDNF, which then create a positive flow-on effect. As the cells in the hippocampus (an area involved with memory storage, consolidation and learning) and the limbic system (the part of the brain involved with emotion processing and behaviour) begin to communicate better and have improved synaptic plasticity, memory and learning increase and, therefore, so does overall mood. You can see how intricately linked all these factors are when it comes to feeling happy or feeling depressed. When you are looking to improve your overall happiness and self-love, it is important to understand how these chemicals can be altered and how they affect different regions of your brain, so you can do something about it.

BDNF can be lost through substance abuse, injury or trauma to the brain, chronic health problems and mood disorders, and genetic and environmental factors also play a role. But there is still a lot to learn about this neurotrophin and why some people have lower levels than others.

How can we increase BDNF in the brain?

Moderate to high-intensity exercise is one of the best ways to increase BDNF within the brain. And yes, studies show that moderate to high-intensity exercise is superior to low-intensity exercise. High-intensity exercise groups show significantly higher levels of BDNF when compared to the lower intensity or stretching groups in a study published by Jeon and Ha in 2017. When the body temperature goes up in intervals, through exercise or sauna use, BNDF goes up overall. Which leads me to saunas and ice baths! These are great tools to not only boost your BDNF but also reduce cortisol levels overall. Doing things to reduce your stress levels, such as improving your sleep (more on that in the chapters on cortisol and stress), are going to help with your BDNF levels too.

12

Dopamine

DOPAMINE IS INVOLVED IN REWARDS PROCESSING AND reward circuitry. It is commonly thought of as the 'motivation' neurotransmitter. It's important for learning and is also crucial for motor skills, motor control and initiation of movement. Dopamine will make you more WILLING to do something and, therefore, will increase your focus and attention. It increases your interest, your curiosity and the likelihood of you exploring things. It will also prompt you to seek out reward, hence why it's known as the motivation chemical.

The brain is always seeking homeostasis, and it is always releasing dopamine to a certain extent. However, a greater amount or a surge of dopamine will get released when you are seeking or anticipating a reward, to encourage you to get that thing or to stay involved with that thing.

You are wired to be motivated to do things that will promote your survival; either direct survival, such as eating and drinking, but also indirect survival, such as reproduction for survival of the species and pro-social behaviours like bonding so you are not kicked out of your community. Anything that leads to these behaviours is likely to give a surge of dopamine, which makes you think, 'That felt good, I want to do it again' or 'I want more of it, right now'. This is why dopamine underlies chemical and behavioural addictions.

When you do get a surge of dopamine, the aftermath is to have a period of little to no dopamine being released. It is released in anticipation of the reward and during the time of experiencing the reward; however, immediately after, you have a short period where there is a deficit of dopamine below baseline before the level recovers.

How dopamine gets depleted

When the release of these chemicals is being manipulated either through chemical or behavioural addictions or habits, the reward system is hijacked. The more you engage in instant reward-seeking behaviour, the bigger the drop below baseline, which then gets you trapped and feeling even more flat. This could explain a lot about your daily levels of motivation. Ever wonder why after you spend so much time on social media and feel compelled to stay on it, scrolling your morning away, you feel quite flat and unmotivated when you get off the apps? You feel like you have no drive, so you then turn to more reward-seeking behaviours that you know will make you feel good. I like to think of them as pacifiers of discomfort. No one likes to try to get mundane tasks done. while they are feeling flat, so you think, I'll do that later when I'm feeling up for it, but in the meantime I'll just jump onto social media again or I'll just raid the fridge for something delicious.

Before the advent of online gambling, social media, text messages and all these tools we now have at our fingertips, it took longer to receive a reward for our actions. Evolution made this seeking of the reward worth it, so we would be bothered enough to follow through. Evolution didn't antici-pate that such a tiny amount of effort would now be what would trigger this reward feeling. This instant-gratification world we live in is not how reward-seeking was designed to be, and having dopamine drop below baseline several times a day is not how we were supposed to experience this neurochemical.

If you are wondering why you never feel like getting to work on your passion project or never get out to exercise or anything else you have set as a goal, this may be what is happening. If you wake up in the morning and the first thing you do is engage in reward-seeking behaviour, such as scrolling through your phone, then you are already bringing your dopamine levels below baseline, before you even get out of bed! Then you expect yourself to go and tackle a morning full of things to do and you wonder what is wrong with you.

Nothing is wrong with you, you just need to learn how to keep the dopamine levels healthy, without these big surges and big lows. If you can do that, then your willingness to do things will return. You will become less distracted because without these big drops you are able to maintain your focus better. That pull to 'get shit done' will be there.

Now that you understand how dopamine goes through these cycles, I want you to look at your day. Look at your behaviours. How often are you setting yourself up for failure? How often do you make it so you are less likely to act on the things that matter to you? The aim here is to not deplete your dopamine levels too much. The release is never steady, nor should it be, but certain actions (ahem, social media use) will deplete your dopamine to the extent that you are not motivated to get up and do something, while other actions keep the levels high enough to keep you feeling up to the task for the whole day.

You have more of a release of dopamine in anticipation of getting what you want, which makes sense because it is what will push you to go and get that thing you want. Once you take part in a behaviour that feels good, your brain then starts to create an association to this conditioned stimulus. A conditioned stimulus is something, anything, that you associate with your reward. For example, a notification sound or symbol is the conditioned stimulus saying something exciting is coming, so your reward circuit identifies it and releases more dopamine to get you to act. The stronger the stimulus and the stronger the dopamine release, the harder it is to not take that action. Look at poker machines and the sounds they make; they are designed to condition people to associate a sound or an image with a reward and they will start to feel the feelings of the reward before they even get it. There are many examples where this happens and you may not even be aware that it is happening to you subconsciously.

If you want to start feeling more driven or motivated, think about reducing instant gratification and reward-seeking behaviour – the kind of thing where the anticipation of getting it is almost more exciting than actually getting it. This is where habits become crucial for your overall drive and happiness: they set your day up for success, keep a healthy cycle of dopamine in your body and encourage you to engage in feel-good activities that are not about chasing a quick reward. I'll be covering habits and routines later on, but keep this in mind when thinking about creating your new routine.

How to increase dopamine in a healthy way

You can see that dopamine can be amazing in the sense that it makes you MOVE. It makes you get off your ass and take action. You just need to harness it for the right reasons and not ones that will leave you feeling flat. Dopamine can also help you delay gratification. It helps you set goals for yourself in the short and long term and it keeps you on track to achieve that goal when you think about it. It is your driving force and, if your goal is something you value enough, it will even help you change your behaviour and your patterns for the better to get you close to that goal. It can even help you resist cravings if you have a desired outcome.

If you have low self-esteem, low self-love, low energy and low focus, it could be down to your dopamine dipping below baseline too much or having an unhealthy dopamine release cycle. And if you feel this way, then you are more likely to go for the quick spikes in dopamine by engaging in instantly gratifying and reward-seeking behaviours. It's not that you are being lazy for no reason, there is a science behind this feeling. Without meaning to, you could be contributing to this vicious cycle. But of course, as with most things, there is something you can do about it.

Given that dopamine is crucial for learning, interest and curiosity, when you start focusing on learning new things, as in personal growth, and seeing improvements in what you are working on, then your dopamine starts to naturally increase and then you are more likely to retain dopamine. When you think about something you love or are interested in, you are able to hold your attention. People who have a purpose and who focus on growth daily are more in the zone, more interested and, therefore, have a better release of dopamine throughout the day.

You want to reduce the impulsive behaviours that, when you do a lot of them, leave you feeling shit. You don't have to eliminate them, just reduce them. If you have a bit of cake, it feels nice, it tastes great and you feel fine. However, if you eat the whole thing, it's not so great anymore. If you spend four minutes on Instagram you feel fine and are still driven to do other tasks; if you spend two hours on it you feel flat because you depleted all your stores and additionally you feel guilty for not doing anything else with your time. So now your bad feelings are twofold; remorse for not being productive and a literal chemical depletion. So simply limit your interaction with these things. Set a timer if you need to. For me, the timer is the best thing. It makes me behave with intention. I am less likely to mindlessly scroll because I know my time on the app is limited.

13

Endorphins

ENDORPHINS ARE KNOWN AS THE BODY'S NATURAL PAIN reliever. They are what is responsible for that 'runner's high' feeling after exercise. The word endorphin means endogenous morphine. Endogenous because it is produced by the body, and morphine because it binds to the same opiate receptor in the central nervous system that morphine binds to, giving that pain relief and euphoric feeling.

Endorphins are neurotransmitters and hormones, and they are a group of three peptides produced in the pituitary gland, which is located at the base of the brain. They are vital for helping us push through pain when necessary (think of when you hurt yourself but must still get to a safe place) or when you need to perform an act of incredible strength in an emergency or to save a life. They help reduce stress so you can deal with the problem at hand. Have you heard of people who have been shot or attacked and don't feel much pain, if any, until they have got themselves to safety?

Pain inhibition is the main effect that endorphins are known for. They can also prevent the release of something called substance P, which is involved in pain signal transmission and is also released when we are stressed. It interacts with the dopamine system by indirectly increasing the release of dopamine. Additionally, when the reward circuit is triggered, endorphins are released along with dopamine.

If endorphin levels are chronically low, there is a higher chance of experiencing depression, anxiety and insomnia.

Low levels are also linked with addiction problems and impulsivity. When endorphin levels are high, they improve your overall wellbeing substantially. Depression, anxiety and mood swings are reduced, your self-esteem goes up, your pain response goes down and your immune system is improved.

Additionally, endorphins get released during exercise, sex, laughter and meditation, and when eating foods that we love or listening to music. When we have a release of endorphins, our tolerance of pain goes up. So you can see here that there are quite a few things you can do to manipulate the levels of endorphins within your system, exercise being the most popular tool.

14

How Cortisol Alters the Brain (Hint: It's Reversible)

What cortisol does

Stress and the production of cortisol play a very critical role in our lives and they can be brilliant or damaging. There are two kinds of stress. The first is acute stress, the good stress. It is when you are responding to a stimulus that incites fear. It is known as the fight or flight response – that adrenaline rush or boost in cortisol – but, additionally, it is what pushes you through stage fright, public speaking or an exam. You get a surge of this chemical to help you perform at your best to get the job done. In these times of heightened stress you are in the zone, acutely aware of what is going on and hyper-focused. This good stress is necessary for avoiding danger, but also for taking on those big moments in life. It is necessary and it is not damaging or detrimental at all, as the cortisol that gets released is absorbed properly and doesn't hang around. If you were to get rid of this kind of stress, you would be disadvantaged. You would not have the heightened awareness or focus needed to get you through the high-pressure moments in your life.

The second kind of stress is mainly what I want to talk to you about. This kind of stress is when you may be easily annoyed or moody, your patience with others is thin, you forget simple things or names or the location of items, you struggle to retain new information, your sleep is not great, or you may feel restless. How does it happen in the first place? There are many things that can cause the onset of chronic stress and most of these things already exist in your life, but if it crosses a threshold then it can tip over to chronic stress. It could be:

- being in an abusive relationship (not just romantically)
- always being under the pump at work and never getting a rest (the feeling of burnout)
- having everyone depend on you and never being able to share the responsibility
- emotional fatigue – going through a difficult time in your life.

This kind of stress is not good because the effects it has on the brain are very different to the effects of acute stress. It literally changes the connectivity between certain brain regions and can shrink certain areas of the brain as well. How insane is that?

It is imperative that you start to put your brain health first. Brain health is crucial for happiness. If you are someone who suffers from chronic stress and you do nothing to stop it, then you may be more susceptible to developing a mood disorder, such as depression, or an anxiety disorder in the future and then, in some cases, neurodegenerative diseases.

What changes occur in the brain during chronic stress?

There is a part of the brain called the hypothalamic pituitary adrenal (HPA) axis and its role is to control your body's response to stress. It releases cortisol for instant response. This happens for both acute and chronic stress. And, as you read in the chapter on serotonin, cortisol also reduces the amount of serotonin available.

If you suffer from chronic stress, way too much cortisol is being released, which is then not being absorbed and metabolised properly. If a higher level of cortisol is being released all the time, then it is harder for you to get a spike of cortisol in those acute moments of fight-or-flight stress. It is the double whammy of feeling stressed all the time, but then not getting the benefits of cortisol when you actually need it.

Higher levels of cortisol will increase activity levels and connectivity between neurons (increased synapses) in an area of the brain called the amygdala. The amygdala is part of a network within the brain called the limbic system. This area is involved in emotion processing and in forging fear-based memories and fearful emotions. If cortisol levels remain high, then the amygdala stays very active and it keeps sending signals of fear or fear responses to what are sometimes neutral stimuli.

Additionally, changes are happening in the hippocampus. This part of the brain is involved in memory and learning, and also in memory consolidation. High levels of cortisol have been found to shrink this brain region. The connectivity and size are reduced, thereby making that area less active. This is why when someone is chronically stressed, their memory isn't crash hot, which can then cause a vicious cycle of stress and irritability because their brain isn't working the way they want it to, but their stressing about it only makes it worse. Can you see the pattern?

This excessive cortisol floating around affects the ability of the HPA axis to regulate itself. This means that it no longer can determine when to crank up the release of cortisol or when to taper it down. It is essentially inhibited and can't regulate itself, so it just continues to release more and more. The more cortisol is released, the less the adrenal axis can perform properly.

All this excessive cortisol then has an effect on synapses between neurons throughout the entire brain. This is when the brain can start to shrink over a long period of time. If this is happening, it is harder to be proactive and positive. Your different brain regions don't communicate as well as they do when you are calm and happy, so it makes it harder to feel good, happy, calm and confident.

The prefrontal cortex

Excessive cortisol also has an effect on the prefrontal cortex. This brain region is responsible for concentration, social interaction, executive function, judgement, decision-making and predicting consequences to your actions. This is the part of the brain that can down-regulate the activity within the limbic system and the amygdala. It is the 'logic' part of the brain that has the ability to override intense reactions or emotions. The more this area is trained (more on that in a sec!), the better you become at being able to chill out, be less reactive and stay calm even in the most intense situations. However, chronic stress (you guessed it) also reduces connectivity between the prefrontal cortex and the limbic system and reduces synapses within these regions as well, therefore the emotional processing area takes over.

This is where interpreting an event will determine how the event is experienced. Take a task that may be challenging, for example. Someone experiencing chronic stress will avoid it, stress over it, worry about not being able to complete it, turn it into a huge insurmountable task in their head, put it off until they can no longer avoid it, cry over it, lose sleep and it takes over their mind. Someone who does not suffer from chronic stress will look at that same task and think, 'Right, how will I tackle this? What section first? Let's break it down'. They instantly switch to problem-solving mode, start working on the task earlier and, therefore, are less likely to be stressed about it. Both people may have the same level of intelligence, but the chronically stressed person will have a harder time allocating their intelligence to the task as they are not functioning at their peak. It comes down to what parts of the brain are taking over when you are working on a task.

The role attachment theory plays in stress levels

It has been shown that the more affectionate a parent is to a baby (physical affection, repair, calming the child down) will determine how that person then goes on to respond to stress. If they were super nurtured, they will be less susceptible to being overly stressed.

A study by Weaver et al. that focused on epigenetic programming in rat models, found that rats whose mothers were super nurturing and caring developed more cortisol receptors, which meant they were able to absorb or use up the available cortisol that was present, so it wasn't floating around the synapse to affect other areas of the brain.

The opposite happened to the rats of non-nurturing mothers. This may explain for some people why they feel they are generally more stressed in everyday tasks than those around them. However, the study showed that when they swapped the stressed group of rats to the nurturing mother, the negative effects on the brain from a chemical and structural level were reversed. It has also been shown that these negative effects can be reversed, with the appropriate behavioural tools, in adults.

15

How to Counter the Effects of Stress

ALL OF THIS INFORMATION ON STRESS AND CORTISOL SOUNDS pretty hectic, right? It is, but understanding this part is actually quite empowering because it explains why some people get set off easier than others and why it feels like a vicious cycle of feeling stressed and feeling powerless. I find it exciting to know that the feelings you feel when you are at your lowest can be explained by physical changes that are happening within your head and that this can be changed.

When you work on reducing stress and the effects it has on your brain, the connectivity and size within areas of your brain changes. The levels of neurochemicals begin to find a better balance and you will become happier, more creative, more connected and calmer. This is the first step to becoming truly happy, so please do not skip it. It can change your life.

There are two fantastic behavioural tools that you can use to overcome the effects of stress on the brain and retrain yourself into a calmer state. These are meditation and exercise. Both these behaviours increase activity in the prefrontal cortex. When you meditate and exercise you promote activity within this area but also connectivity between the prefrontal cortex and the limbic system and hippocampus. The more connected these areas are, the more influence the reasoning part of the brain has over the reactive, fearful or emotional part of the brain.

Additionally, your hippocampus increases in size, which is heavily associated with learning and memory consolidation. As this area becomes more active, you are then able to retain more and retrieve more.

16

Why the Brain Procrastinates

BELIEVE IT OR NOT, PROCRASTINATION CAN IMPACT YOUR relationship with yourself. It is an avoidance mechanism that can cause you to start avoiding things that are necessary for you to progress in life. If you get in the way of your growth because you didn't act, then you blame yourself, feel bad about yourself, the narratives you tell yourself are ugly and your self-love is impacted. Sometimes you may find that it is an insurmountable challenge to change your thoughts, feel good about yourself or stress less when your brain has been operating a certain way for such a long time. The following may help you find clarity and understanding as to why your brain may be wired in an anxious, stressful or reactive way; why it seems to get worse and worse; and, most of all, how it can be changed.

I think you may by now be picking up on a theme here; your brain is the way it is due to how you have conditioned it or how it has been conditioned. Many factors are at play, but it is not by chance that you think or react the way you do. Your brain believes that this is how it is, that this way of thinking will serve you best. So, unless you retrain it, it will keep telling you certain things.

Discomfort is subjective. You ultimately can decide what is uncomfortable, comfortable and neutral. And for many things, what starts out as uncomfortable can become pleasant or even enjoyable, like exercise, waking up early, even cleaning (imagine such a thing)! It's all about how you approach it. But WHY do we avoid things in the first place?

Wouldn't it be easier to be able to like something from the get-go?

The moment you think something will represent discomfort, your mind will choose the more comfortable option, unless you challenge it.

You avoid discomfort for one of two reasons:

1. There is a better option in front of you.
2. You are fearful of the unknown, so you pick the lesser evil (what you DO know).

Every time you avoid something, it is due to these reasons. Discomfort can come in all shapes and forms: pain, boredom, effort (mental and physical), anxiety, potential rejection, and judgement of others. When you avoid the unknown, it's generally because you are predicting one of these things to happen. There is physical discomfort – not wanting to do the work because relaxing is the preferred option available. Or there is emotional discomfort – not wanting to put yourself out there because it could mean embarrassment, failure or rejection.

But the thing is that this discomfort always feels worse when you are avoiding it or thinking about it. You have all this mental capacity to think up all the bad that could happen or all the things to be fearful of while you are in the safe place of not taking action. If you were to start, you wouldn't have nearly as much energy available to dedicate to thinking about the worst-case scenario. You would be too busy taking action. DOING the thing. And once you do start, once you commit, it's rarely as bad as you anticipate because you are distracted with the task at hand. It's not possible to now dedicate so much focus to complaining about it. Your conscious mind is too busy for that shit.

We hesitate because our fear circuit – our limbic system – is pulling the brakes. It's telling you, 'Whoa! Don't go there. You can't handle that! Look over here! Look at this safe and comfortable option instead – let's go there!' Hesitation is pausing because you are uncertain or scared of something. It is due to the fear of the unknown, or the knowledge of it being unpleasant and requiring hard work or patience. Only a quick intervention of thoughts can stop this pattern. And that intervention must happen BEFORE you give yourself a chance to talk yourself out of it. Like attracts like, so if you think one bad thought, it's going to snowball. If you think, I'll make that uncomfortable phone call in ten minutes, then you will be so worked up, have created so many reasons why it may be a bad idea or why it will go wrong, that by the time you make that phone call, you are either too scared or you can barely get your words out. If you hesitate but then quickly override that thought and take action, you will have thought up less factors or possibilities to be scared of. You are now focusing on the task at hand and are less likely to get caught up in your anxiety.

17

What Happens in the Brain When You Are Feeling Shit

THE NEUROSCIENCE OF SELF-LOVE

WHEN YOU ARE FEELING DOWN, YOU SEEK OUT PACIFIERS AND distractions. You reach for things that make you stop feeling so flat, but these external pacifiers are almost always quick fixes. It is a bandaid fix to something that is asking for attention. You can't work on your self-love if every time your mind, emotions and body are trying to tell you something you go and brush it under the rug and place a distraction over it. Pacifiers and distractions often aren't things that slowly regulate our neurochemicals. They are the social media checking or having a drink, cigarette or vape; those things that have a chemical reaction within our brain due to a substance or a behaviour that gives us that instant feel-good reward. Now that you understand how dopamine works in your system, you can understand why you can feel so flat but still proceed to spend your whole day online or doing things that you know the you of tomorrow will feel even worse about. So don't feel guilty, there is a science behind this madness. But it's definitely something you may want to look into changing because, although you may not have wanted to cause it, it will only keep you in a loop of feeling flat and unproductive and then probably engaging in negative self-talk. Let's change that.

These are the typical pacifiers that people normally turn to, although you may have your own special preference:

- social media
- TV
- betting or gambling

- shopping (online or in person)
- games that turn your attention elsewhere.

These things alone are fine but, when used to replace your low mood, can be detrimental and can cause an even bigger slump – that remorseful feeling – and it will encourage you to keep engaging in these behaviours to avoid sitting in silence because, for many, sitting in silence with their own thoughts causes them to spiral into anxious or fearful thoughts or destructive self-talk.

This cycle rarely ends by itself. It's when you find yourself year in, year out setting the same goals and resolutions only to find yourself at the end of the year wondering where the time went and why you didn't get things done. This then perpetuates the problem because you may be feeling guilty or frustrated with yourself and that only encourages the cycle to repeat itself.

How do you snap out of feeling low?

Accept and forgive

First of all, accept, forgive and repair (more on repair in the coming chapter). What's done is done. The time you have spent is gone. Acceptance of the now and what you can do with the now is what will change your focus from beating yourself up for wasting time to what you can do right now, this afternoon or tonight.

Help the you of tomorrow

If I have had a super unproductive day, I will try to do something, anything, before I go to bed that will help my tomorrow self. I will make sure my home is tidy or I will plan out the structure of my week so I am more prepared. I will get my workout stuff ready for the morning. Just the tiniest thing that you need to do will shift your focus. Once it is done, you feel less anxious and less likely to go back to pacifying behaviours.

Get back to baseline

In these moments when you feel the flattest, when you are most pulled to distract or pacify yourself, that is when you want to step away from these behaviours, so you don't feel worse. Almost like a cleanse for the mind. You want to give yourself a time out and replace it with something else. Go for a walk, read a book, go hang out with a friend or call someone to chat – do things that make you either feel relaxed or connected. Notice how these things all require a certain amount of focused effort in a low-stimulation environment and are not passive. Reading a book is calming, not highly stimulating and requires focus. Conversely, watching TV is a lot more passive and highly stimulating with the sounds, colours and vast amount of information being thrown your way; this is going to trigger a higher spike in dopamine and leave you wanting even more. And look out for things where you are seeking a reward like in the list of pacifiers at the start of this chapter; avoiding them will start to bring your dopamine levels back up to normal, where you are getting a natural release without feeling depleted.

18

The Importance of Repair

AN EXERCISE THAT YOU CAN DO IS TO LOOK AT THE THOUGHTS you harbour in your mind and try to choose to entertain new thoughts. The more you do this the better you get at it AND the better you feel. And just like training or eating well, consistency is what matters, not perfection. Perfection is just a form of procrastination; you look at this seemingly unattainable goal and think, well I couldn't do it perfectly so why try? It is your mind telling you to just put it off until you are ready because it is avoiding discomfort. So let's get rid of the idea of being perfect and let's start now.

When you train, if you do so each day for a few weeks and then you miss one day, not much is going to happen, especially if you get back on track. The same goes for the hard work you have put in with self-love. You can be doing all the work and then an incident happens that causes you to feel bad about yourself or you go through a breakup or have a fight with someone. You start to feel all these negative thoughts come crashing down on you and, in that moment, it feels as if all the work you have done has been for nothing. Right? The mind is a crafty tool and it loves to spiral. So next time this happens, just understand it is the mind doing its thing. The truth is that your success lies in how you repair things with yourself. How you rewrite and repair those thoughts and conversations you have had with yourself.

Everyone has their bad days, but those who are confident and truly love themselves have an ability to be understanding and patient with themselves and, most of all, be sympathetic. They may have their moments where they spiral downwards but, instead of beating themselves up about it and slipping back into old habits, they spend some time repairing by overwriting bad thoughts with neutral or positive thoughts, by calming down, and by doing specific exercises that help relax themselves and soothe the over-active emotional centres in their brain. And before they know it, the repair is done and they are back on track. Notice the difference? Neither the confident people nor the insecure people are perfect. Both groups slip up and both groups have their bad days and have bad things happen.

Your focus should only ever be on overall consistency and the ability to repair. Just like I spoke about the repair between the parent and child in the attachment theory chapter, this is what is now happening between you and your mind. The principles from your early years and how you approached struggles and conflict apply to your life now. You may even begin to understand why it is that you have been so hard on yourself in the past, possibly because you never learnt the importance of repair in the first place, before you continue on with your daily routine.

If you were to imagine that you had scolded a child, or even a sibling or best friend, what would be your initial reaction? Ideally you would first reflect on what was said, then you would decide if it was appropriate or not and, if not, you would take steps to apologise, mend the relationship by offering support and warmth, and then after the apology you would say things to override what you had originally done or said to reaffirm how you truly feel towards that person or what you truly think about them. The other person would then calm down, drop their walls and open up to you and listen to what you say. The repair has been done and the connection is strong again. This is EXACTLY how you want the cycle of repair to work with yourself. You want to mirror the bond between a parent and child who have a secure attachment.

The more you do this, the easier it will be to bounce back and the less often you will need to do it. At first what can be difficult to do, such as being warm and understanding and apologising to yourself, will soon enough become second nature.

What happens if you don't do the repair? Well, you may be looking at the result of that right now. You engage in more negative self-talk, you doubt yourself and your abilities, you expect less of yourself and, due to this, you attempt things less. You become more cautious in your actions and you are less likely to dare to dream. Based on this, you then form a strengthened belief of who you are, what love you are deserving of receiving (based on this current love that you give yourself) and you also form a belief of what you are capable of achieving. The cycle then continues. As you expect less of yourself, you expect less from others and you continue to disappoint yourself. Some of you may resonate with this as it is the only way you have ever been. But it is something that can be rewritten with practice, just like daily exercise.

How do you start repairing?

You can start right now, understanding that you will slip back into those old thoughts more often than you would like. When you understand that REPAIR must come before change happens, then you will hopefully place more importance on it and dedicate more time to it. It doesn't have to be a tragic, long-winded emotional rollercoaster you go on. On the contrary, you are removing the neurotic mental chat, slowing it down and becoming more present.

You are pausing, looking at what you did, then (without being judgemental of yourself) you are apologising, offering comfort (by slowing down, taking time off) and then giving yourself three or more reasons or sentences that override what you said or did to yourself.

Don't wait for a bad day to do the repair. You can start right now! Pick one thing that you thought you were too hard on yourself for. Just one. And go through those steps to apologise and repair, and then let it go. Don't fester, don't wallow, don't attach too much thought or emotion. We are trying to lighten the load here, not add to it. Do this often and, before you know it, it will start to happen automatically and, even better, you will identify when you need to stop and repair much faster than usual, so you won't be spiralling for as long.

EXERCISE

Choose one thing to repair and forgive yourself for now.

Write it down and tell yourself why you forgive yourself and why you deserve to let it go. Talk to yourself (or write to yourself) the way you would speak to your best friend, not how you are used to speaking to yourself.

Being compassionate with yourself instead of critical is more likely to help you get back on track faster and have a higher chance at success. When we are critical, we may think, 'Oh well, I like to push myself. I am my hardest critic so I know I will get the most out of myself'. But sometimes this criticism gets too much and that is when perfectionism, hesitation and procrastination creep in. It is no longer remotely enjoyable, so we start to avoid it. If you are compassionate, you start to realise that, no matter the outcome, it's going to be fine, so you then feel like you have less to lose. You won't feel like a failure, and you won't think less of yourself, so you are more likely to be able to throw yourself back into the challenge and just see how you go. There is less pressure, so you have more fun doing it and because of this you are more creative with your work. Notice how a simple shift in mindset will get you to a place that previously you had been trying to get to by being critical, yet you missed the mark every time.

19

Riding the Reset Button

EVERY DAY YOU WAKE UP WITH A CLEAN SLATE. THE MIND wakes up neutral; you then choose what to fill it with. Choose wisely. Some people are able to create transformative change within their lives, career or relationships in the span of a day. This normally happens when a major event has occurred that has forced them into a massive shift. For some, they have what they consider to be 'a defining moment', something that really rang out to them telling them that their life needed to change. When this happens it is like you have a massive reset; you are not focused on the past or being nostalgic, you become entrenched in the moment and what is possible or necessary for you, and nothing gets in your way. Whether it be that you instantly stop missing your ex, or you decide to drop everything and move to a different country, or you decide from one day to the next that your personality will be one where you don't take shit from anyone and you begin to exude strength and confidence because you are sick of being walked all over. This kind of thing is possible for anyone to achieve. Not common, but possible.

However, for most people that is not the case. Most of us are in this constant ping-pong game with two versions of ourselves. One is the past self and the other is the present self who is aware of the possibilities of our own future, who is pulling us to move forward. Severing the tie from your old self, old behaviours and old habits is not easy when you are still thinking the same way and when the circumstances you are creating around yourself are not changing.

This is what happens in our minds when we create a habit. We are entrenched in a way of being and that way has been repeated over and over. We have strengthened that pathway so much in our brains that it then becomes subconscious. When something is subconscious it requires almost no effort and, even more importantly, we do it whether we want to or not, and the only way to counteract this habit is through conscious presence. Presence is the only way to pierce through the noise of the mind.

There are a few ways to override those pathways in the brain. One way is through an intense emotional experience; this could be trauma or PTSD, where suddenly your behaviours and way of thinking can change, or it could be something positive, such as a great realisation or an awakening to a new level of understanding. The other way, and this is what we are going to focus on in this chapter, is through repetitive actions and thought patterns. If done often enough and if enough energy is sent to these new pathways, they become stronger and the old pathways receive less attention, less use and less nutrition so they start to get weaker and weaker.

I want you to remind yourself of this fact every time you are attempting something new. Each morning, each HOUR can be a reset for yourself. And every time you hit that reset button, no matter how many times, you are placing effort and attention into new and different connections within your brain and taking them away from the old subconscious habits that do not serve you anymore.

So, regardless of how many attempts you make, do not let that bring you down; if you understand the physical changes that are unfurling beneath the surface of your brain you will understand that no attempt is futile. The only thing you want to focus on is being prepared to show up again, no matter how many times you reset. Don't hold any resistance to the notion of 'failure'. That is just a concept that we have created and attached a huge amount of meaning and emotion to. If you remove the label of failure, it loses its power. Your focus should remain only on what it is that you are doing now, in the present moment, at the next attempt, the next reset. And before you know it, small, tiny changes will turn into powerful habits and rituals that you no longer will need to push yourself to do.

20

How to Rewrite Your Cognitive Distortion

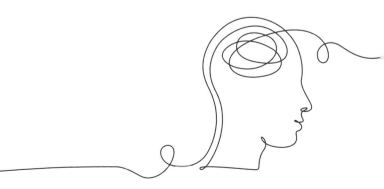

What is cognitive distortion?

Cognitive distortion is an irrational thought pattern that normally happens during states of anxiety or depression. It causes you to inaccurately perceive reality or predict a scenario by only thinking of a negative outcome. I am going to go over some of the more common forms of cognitive distortion that can be quite toxic for your own thought patterns and narratives about yourself.

Catastrophising

Catastrophising is thinking of the worst-case scenario. Not just being aware of it, but predicting that the worst is about to happen. It stops people from going to a job interview, speaking up at a social event, telling their crush they like them, addressing a difficult topic with someone close to them, moving house and so much more. The more you catastrophise, the more you avoid situations. This avoidance will likely increase your anxiety around these situations. You build it up to be something so big that you don't want to address it. You begin to doubt your every move; you become self-critical, less creative, less spontaneous and, as a result, you end up suffering in your career and your relationships. This takes a toll on your mental health and you can see how catastrophising can become a vicious cycle that gets harder and harder to get out of. This is an example of where the amygdala and limbic system take over and the prefrontal cortex doesn't have a chance to override these thoughts due to high levels of chronic stress.

Generalising

This is where you make universal or general statements about yourself or others. Often the more anxious or insecure you are about a topic, the more you generalise and make sweeping statements. We want to replace these universal statements with specific statements. For example, if you fail one exam, you may say, 'I am such a failure, why did I bother? Everything is so hard for me'. A replacement statement would be, 'I feel I wasn't prepared for that exam and I failed it this time. I am capable of passing the exam if I prepare for the questions I struggled with. I am capable of studying and learning things even if it is at a slower pace than others'. There are many alternative phrases you could create.

The same thing goes for making sweeping statements about things outside of you. If you generalise, then the chances of you seeing the good in a person or situation are slim. If you say, 'All men are assholes', then you already have this idea that in order for you to like a man, he has to PROVE that he breaks that idea in your head. You have an idea of what someone is and, instead of learning about them, you pass early judgement based on what others have done. This goes for communities, nationalities, genders, age groups and so on. It's a good idea to start to question these ideas every time you generalise. Is this a true statement? How much evidence do I have to back this generalisation? When we generalise like this, it is our mind using cognitive bias in a really detrimental way. It stops us not only from believing we can do more, but also from forming connections with new people or seeing the good in people we may have prejudged.

Mind-reading

One of the most anxiety-provoking things you can do is to engage in mind-reading and presume what others are thinking or feeling about you or a situation that involves you. You can work yourself up thinking of all the horrible things someone is thinking of you and then, because you believe it so wholeheartedly, you approach them and the situation differently. You look at a neutral reaction and take it as a bad reaction. If someone is quiet, you think they are annoyed at YOU. If two of your friends are laughing, you think they are laughing at something you did. This can then escalate into imagining that someone is mad at you or doing things behind your back, which then prompts you to seek assurance from that person that they do in fact like you, or that they aren't mad at you or that you have not done something wrong. This can get very exhausting for friends or partners and actually does nothing to soothe your insecurities. It only makes them worse. Every time someone pacifies your insecurities it makes you feel validated. For that very short moment, you feel heard and loved, and that back and forth of fear and reassurance can be quite addictive, despite the fact that the reward does not outweigh the suffering.

Thinking everything is your fault

This is a way of making everything about YOU (negatively). You look at what is happening in other peoples' lives and somehow take an unrelated event and think you caused it. If your boss is short-tempered or your friend doesn't reply, you think it is because of something you did.

Imagine a scenario where you are going to meet up with a friend, and that friend doesn't show. You try calling them and there's no answer. After an hour of waiting, you leave. For most, the initial thought would be they are in traffic, which might then lead to thinking that they lost their phone or forgot, and then this thought process may even turn to worry, hoping that they are okay. However, for someone who thinks everything is their fault, their initial reaction would be to think that they did something wrong and that now this friend is punishing them by not showing up and ignoring their calls. There are a million things that could be the reason for something happening, but in this style of cognitive distortion, it somehow gets turned into being your fault, regardless of there being no evidence to back your belief.

EXERCISE

How do we stop irrational thoughts?

We don't. We redirect them, we redirect that energy. If you find yourself engaging in any of the previous thought patterns, try the following.

Record, rationalise and replace.

- **Record:** Write it down and explain in detail what happened, how you felt and how you initially reacted to it. Start a daily journal to address these thought patterns. At the end of the day, write down what you avoided, what catastrophic thoughts you had. Record all your feelings and what scenarios went through your head. Write it all down.
- **Rationalise:** Next to each statement, write down ways of rationalising this thought or reaction that you had. Ask yourself, is this true? How likely is it that this will be the outcome? Come up with counter thoughts or questions that challenge yourself and label what you are doing here. Are you catastrophising? Are you generalising? Is there enough evidence to back this statement? Is this a true statement? Or a guess?
- **Replace:** Then last of all, replace it with a new thought. The more often you do this, the faster you can intercept and replace these irrational

thoughts. As you get used to doing this, your initial reactions to circumstances will get less and less extreme until you can start having positive reactions or neutral reactions to what normally would have been a mood-killing reaction for you, one that would ruin your day.

An example of a replacement

If your catastrophising thought was, 'I can't bring up this issue with my partner because they will get defensive, and then it will be my fault and they will threaten to leave me for accusing them of something', you could replace that statement with, 'I want to give my partner a chance to discuss this openly with me. They deserve it and so do I. I can't predict what will happen. I will allow it to unfold'. By doing this more and more, you will stop assuming what the future outcome will be and, therefore, you will be less defensive and more likely to be open-minded.

When you are feeling down on yourself and when you talk down to yourself, the language you use can be extremely detrimental and often linked to extreme emotion. Statements like, 'I shouldn't have done that. I am so embarrassed. Everyone thinks I'm an idiot. I can never go there again. What is wrong with me? I am such a failure', are quite catastrophic and anxiety provoking, and can only result in you feeling worse about yourself or engaging in avoidance behaviours. You become less confident within yourself, less comfortable in your own skin and less likely to take risks and put yourself out there.

Reducing such thoughts by doing these exercises will start to increase your self-esteem, confidence and self-love. These tools are taken from cognitive behavioural therapy exercises and are ways of rewriting your internal working model; how you view yourself, others and the world. Self-talk is one of the things that heavily influences what your relationship to yourself is like. When you identify these cognitive distortions and do the exercises around them, you will literally start to change which areas of your brain are dominant when responding to something. Just like a muscle, you will train your thoughts and brain to eventually think this way automatically.

21

The Many Versions of YOU

IDENTITY IS A HUGE PART OF CONFIDENCE AND HOW YOU FEEL about yourself. Sometimes we get so wrapped up in our identity and what we project forward that, if we don't live up to that particular image, we feel we have failed ourselves. This can impact how you feel about yourself and, of course, your self-love. What if you could compartmentalise different versions of you? You are not a two-dimensional image, so your personality shouldn't be either. When you pigeonhole yourself into one category, you limit yourself to just that and are less likely to be receptive to other opportunities, and are also less likely to be spontaneous and listen to what you truly want.

If you keep saying, 'I'm so social. I don't like being alone. I need busy busy busy!' then you are more likely to feel weird staying in, thinking that you are alone instead of having 'me' time. You will avoid things that slow you down, such as meditation or sitting with your own thoughts and, before you know it, you will have just dismissed all these things that may make you feel good because they don't align with the concept you have of yourself.

You don't have to put forth all the attributes you possess at all times. You can express many different things at different times and these things can be contrasting. Look at it as being multifaceted. And you need to give attention to each version of you in order to feel heard by you.

Some examples of these versions are: a quiet self; a loud, social self who wants to be out and the life of the party; an affectionate, loving, nurturing, cuddling self; a curious, learning, exploring self; and a badass boss version of yourself. You pick the versions that resonate with you (these ones are my main ones). Sometimes when I'm feeling flat, I think, what version of me do I miss or need to tap into? What version do I need to give attention to to fill my cup? This will help you step away from the constraints of the labels that you have given yourself or that others have given you, and it feels really good to listen to what you or your body needs. It's amazing how rarely we ask ourselves what we need in that moment; we just charge on and ignore what we truly need. It may be silence, a break, an adventure, time with a friend or to sit outside with a book.

EXERCISE

Write down all the different versions of you that you know need attention.

Now identify which one you neglect the most.

Then write down what you could do each week to nurture each version of you and try to incorporate these nurturing activities into your day or week.

Knowing the different versions of yourself also allows you to separate aspects of your life and KEEP them separate. It helps you get into your work zone without feeling like you must be the nurturing version. You can then go out and let your hair down without feeling you must have your shit together. You can even give them different names, to represent each facet of your personality. This compartmentalising helps remove guilt for not giving more of yourself during certain times in your life.

Stop pigeonholing yourself. It is these unnecessary expectations that keep you in a state of not feeling like you are enough or give you low self-worth, which gives you more reasons to put yourself down. This idea that you have to uphold all these responsibilities and all these facets of yourself is something that has been created externally, but nothing outside of you can make you feel the feelings of worthiness. Understanding that you are multifaceted will help you break away from these labels and it will also help you explore parts of you and your personality that maybe you have wanted to have or be but felt that it 'just wasn't you' so you held back. I'm telling you now, anything can be you. You just have to say the word. Any outfit, any activity, any decision. If it comes from you, it is you. Nothing anyone says can determine that for you. It's internal. When you fully grasp this, you let go of this false pressure that exists and you allow yourself to just be and explore the possibilities that exist for you.

So often the reason you might not want to do something different or try something new is because other people will judge you; judge you for doing something out of the 'box' that doesn't fit in to the image that they have of you in their head. But the people around you only get a limited insight into your life and personality. Imagine not following an idea or goal because you are afraid to rock this false image in someone's mind of you that doesn't even reflect you. Get rid of the labels. Get rid of the notion of 'that's not me' or 'I could never do that'. You either want to or you don't; nothing else should determine if you are going to take action or not.

Tap into sides of you that you haven't really given much thought or attention to. You may find that you are more adventurous than you gave yourself credit for, or you have an introverted side that loves doing things alone every so often and that is what grounds you. All these things contribute to your feelings of self-love, because they bring you into the present moment. They get you focusing on what it is that you need in that moment and put you as the priority.

22

Teach People How to Treat You

ONE OF THE THINGS THAT IS CRITICAL TO SELF-LOVE AND confidence is your ability to have your own back and trust your decisions, and to do these knowing that, regardless of the outcome, you will be more than okay. However, if you are used to always explaining yourself and having people question your choices or how you do things, then doubt may start to creep in, especially if boundaries have not yet been set.

When you explain yourself, people take that as an invitation to turn what you are doing into a discussion. They feel like you have welcomed them to do so. Keep in mind, this is not out of malice. Most people do it out of love and most people give their opinions or try to get you to do what they want you to do because they think it is the best choice for you, but they are speaking from their own perspective and their own experience.

Unless you are sure about your decisions, discussing them with people left, right and centre can leave you feeling doubtful and uneasy. You start to question yourself, if it's a safe idea, the risks involved and, before you know it, you are back in the land of procrastination, where everything and everyone passes you by as you sit there and worry about the risks or not being perfect.

My advice to you is to stop feeling the need to explain yourself and asking too many people for advice on your life. Here are the criteria I use.

Firstly, if the matter directly involves the person you are talking to – for example, a decision about where you are living and you are talking to your partner – then you owe that person an explanation. Or if you have done something that has caused a problem with your partner then it is a good idea to explain yourself for the sake of the relationship (obviously). However, if the matter only directly impacts you (for example, your career, how you spend your own money) and only indirectly affects someone else (that person may not want you to go away because they will miss you, hence them feeling impacted, or your parents don't want you to dump that person because they like them for you), then you need to seriously think about why you are explaining yourself.

Secondly, do you have an overwhelming desire to explain yourself? If the answer is no, then don't. Simple. Will people find this weird? Probably. Most people around you feel some level of access to you, an entitlement to tell you what's what and an expectation that you will take their advice because they think they know better than you. But that is not your problem and you want to distance yourself from caring about this as much as possible. You are the one who determines how much access people have to your life and your decisions, no matter how awkward the situation may feel to you. The sooner you start to let people know that they don't have unbridled access to your life, decisions and time, the sooner you will start loving yourself.

It is your job to teach people how to treat you. Don't let them assume and don't hope that they will learn boundaries or read your mind when you want space. You must make that clear and you have to be the one to set that line. If you don't, then everyone will treat you the way THEY see fit, instead of how YOU see fit. If you don't set a standard, they will go by the standard that they feel is acceptable.

When doing this, try to not get annoyed, put your walls up or get upset or anxious. People are going to ask because they are curious and they are going to tell you what to do and offer advice because they think it helps – they really do – and, in most cases, their intentions are good. Just remind yourself, 'This person just hasn't grasped my boundaries yet, so there is no point getting upset when it has nothing to do with me'. This will help you stay calm for when you do implement a bit of a boundary.

When setting a boundary, less is more. You don't have to go into crazy detail as to why you need a boundary; that defeats the purpose. If it feels better for you to explain, then go for gold. But the point is to demonstrate that your actions and decisions are yours and that you choose the level of access that someone has in your life.

Another helpful thing to do is watch how you are with other people. If you expect others to take your advice or to have to explain everything they do when you disagree with them, or if you are judgemental of others, then it will be harder to create your own boundary because you don't want to be hypocritical. Always start by watching your own behaviour. Always. It's easy to see when others cross the line and even easier to ignore it when you do it. So be accountable; show others that you can respect their boundaries and that way you feel more comfortable setting boundaries of your own.

23

Choose What Is Important Over What Is Urgent

ONE OF THE BEST WAYS TO LOVE YOURSELF IS TO DEMON- strate often that you are a priority, that what you want matters. If you always push that aside and are spreading yourself too thin trying to keep up, then you are probably going to feel judgemental or critical. When self-love is low, seeing other people doing what makes them happy and succeeding will be difficult because you will be constantly comparing yourself to them and probably being pretty harsh on yourself in this comparison as well. And then when you are in a position of comparisons and competition, you are less likely to feel driven, passionate and in a flow state. What is a flow state? The term was coined by psychologist Mihaly Csikszentmihalyi, who described 'flow' as a 'highly focused mental state conducive to productivity'. So, like so many other examples I have given you, it is a cycle that keeps feeding itself. You need to break that cycle through conscious action.

Start by looking at your daily to do-list. How do you structure it? What do you deem necessary? Most people will do either all the small, quick jobs or the urgent jobs first in the day – things like emails and returning calls. Once all of this is done, you then allow yourself to dedicate that time to your side passion or side hustle, exercising or a hobby. But I want you to restructure that. If you do all the urgent things first and the things that matter to you later, then you will NEVER get to the things that matter. You will never feel ready to take that leap because you yourself have not prioritised that thing, so you feel unprepared. This can be applied to your tasks at home and at work because it will impact your performance.

Each day you have a decision-making quota. The further along in the day you get, the more effort it takes to make a decision. This is known as decision fatigue, which is a concept that was derived from the strength model of self-control, proposed by Baumeister et al. in 1998. The main idea behind this concept of decision fatigue is that humans have a limit to how much self-control they can administer in a day and the more we have to self-regulate, the more depleted our resources for self-control become, making it harder to make decisions, process information and perform tasks. So, if you do all the quick and easy jobs at the start of the day to get them out of the way, you then have to deal with the jobs that require effort and creativity when you are now fatigued. The more things you can do the night before to prepare for the morning, the fresher you will be to focus on the things that matter. This is why routines are so important. By turning a conscious effort into something subconscious that you don't need to think about or make decisions about, then you can use your decision-making quota on other things.

If you wanted to write a book or start your own business and you left it to the end of the day to work on it, how well do you think it would go? Start to dedicate the first half hour or hour of the day, if you can, to the thing that is most important to you. The thing that gets you excited – your dreams and passions. The earlier in the day, the better – you want to do this with a fresh mind, no matter how little you get done – and make this part of your daily habit. Not only will your mind be at its freshest, meaning you will actually start making some headway on this passion of yours, but you will also start to respect yourself more. You start the day by giving to yourself. Giving your time and your sharpest mind to you instead of handing it out to everyone else until you are exhausted. When you stop giving yourself the leftovers of your energy and time, you start loving yourself more.

Now you may be thinking, 'I am most creative at night! How is this possible?' This normally happens if you are either a night owl who prefers to wake up later as well, or it can also be the case if you have had some downtime in the afternoon to replenish your mind to then access your work at night-time. You can break up your day with a nap, a walk, a dip in a pool or the ocean, or just relaxing in general to give your mind a break. If this is the case for you, great, but if you have depleted your decision-making quota and energy stores with no rest, then you are likely to struggle to stay focused and get a lot of meaningful work done.

Don't kid yourself and say, 'When I have a full day I will work on that thing'. Even if you did dedicate a day off to it, it is not consistent, it is not teaching yourself that you are prioritising this, and you will then drop the ball until the next full day. It has to become a part of your current daily reality for it to stick. You have to raise your standards on how you treat yourself and take daily action.

Lastly, get strict on what is urgent. Some things may obviously be urgent, like submitting a piece of work by a deadline or attending a meeting that cannot be rescheduled. Fine. But be clear on the difference between urgent and something that someone needs you to do for them but isn't actually urgent. Just because your boss tells you it is urgent, it doesn't necessarily mean it is, especially if they are saying every task is urgent. Ask yourself, why is this urgent? What makes this task more important than other tasks? Is it so necessary that I do this first, and why? Sometimes deadlines and schedules are put into place without your input and you may have to challenge them in order to get the important things done.

If you need to rest or take some time off to socialise, that is your decision. Don't let others guilt you into feeling bad for taking time off or going out socialising when you have a lot of work on. Your time off is your time off. If you don't honour that, you will struggle to be happy. You and your time will feel owned by others. Take that ownership back and start getting clear that time off is time off. Urgent things are not all the things that people want from you, but maybe just a fraction of those things, and the things that matter the most to you will get your attention for at least thirty minutes every day. Do yourself this favour and your self-love will start to increase day by day.

24

Honour Your Commitments

WHEN YOU CAN START TO PROVE THINGS TO YOURSELF AND stick to your own promises to yourself, you start to change these automatic thought patterns. You start to create more examples to show yourself that you are in fact capable, resilient and in a position of power. The good thing is that these promises do not have to be big for you to start to feel good about yourself.

Own your mistakes

Making mistakes and owning them is a good thing; it helps you know where you can improve. If you put the blame on others for not keeping you accountable, or for conditions not being perfect as the reason why you didn't try something or go and work out or stick to your meal plan then you will feel less empowered. In an attempt to feel less guilty for not doing something, we make take the power away from ourselves. You need to stop believing that all these external factors are responsible for not sticking to your daily tasks and habits.

Yes, sometimes things happen that are out of your control, but most of the time the reason you may not take consistent action is within your control. If something gets in the way, it shouldn't affect the overall outcome because you have your own consistency backing you up – all the work you have done up until now.

When you take ownership of your slip-ups, you take ownership of your successes. It means you can have the power to change, edit or do something completely different. Look at taking ownership as a blessing and from now on learn to pull yourself up every time you blame the fact that you didn't take action on some external factor. Take responsibility in order to take action. This is not a blame game. Remove blame entirely. Just focus on what you can do (if anything) differently next time. And if you can't change it, then it was never in your control in the first place. If you had planned to go for a run in the morning and then it rained, you may say, 'I meant to exercise but I can't control the weather'. But that could change to saying, 'I meant to run, but instead I did a quick workout on a mat at home. It's not what I had planned, but I found a way to stay on track'.

Another example would be if you had intended to go to the gym, but you had to stay late at work, so it was not physically possible for you to train. In this scenario, even when there is no alternative and you were not able to do the session you promised yourself, you are at peace knowing that, in more cases than not, you have stepped up and honoured your commitment to yourself, so on the occasion that you can't, you don't beat yourself up about it because it truly was a time when you were not able to control the situation.

People who are generally consistent don't beat themselves up when they miss a day or a two because, overall, it doesn't affect them. Only those who consistently find reasons to let themselves down will beat themselves up about it and feel bad later. Find the balance. Perfection doesn't exist, but genuine excuses for you not being able to do something every single day probably don't exist either. It's the middle ground that I want you to find, so you can honour your integrity with yourself and feel great about it.

Have self-integrity

Self-integrity is the most important kind of integrity; when you harness it and it matters to you, you can direct your energy to almost anything. It's no good having integrity for things that are external to you but none for yourself, because then you end up letting yourself down, putting things off and never listening to what your inner self is wanting.

So what does integrity mean exactly? According to the *Oxford English Dictionary* it is:

- the quality of being honest and having strong moral principles
- the state of being whole and undivided.

EXERCISE

If you take this meaning of the word integrity and apply it to yourself, it would mean following through with a plan you have made for yourself, a goal, an exercise, a commitment to changing certain thought patterns. So how do you have MORE integrity?

You start small – in fact, the smaller the better initially – and you honour it. Pick one thing, one thing you already know you are capable of, one thing that is good for your body or mind and try it for seven days straight no matter what.

Starting small is the best way to do it. You lower your expectations initially, to give yourself a good starting base. From there, the sky is the limit with what you can do, but you need to start small. You need to plant the seed and water and nurture it, and before you know it, this seed has grown into something bigger than you could have hoped for. But it can't happen the other way around. Why? When you already are plagued with negative or harmful automatic thoughts and you set out to do something huge, the likelihood of you sticking it out when you encounter a challenge are slim to none. You will feel horrible, feel like a failure and, instead of jumping back on the bandwagon, you'll throw in the towel.

And then the next time you want to embark on something big, you refer to the last time you tried something big, you remember the feeling and then you paint your future with the brush of the past. It's your internal working model, your belief system around what you are capable of, that will determine if you start something new or not. So do yourself a favour and start small. And don't get me wrong, I am your biggest advocate for doing big things, for having big goals and making big changes, but, if you are always doubting yourself, please try small steps first. And don't worry if you are impatient. Small things pick up momentum and don't stay small for long. As you gain momentum, you gain confidence in your abilities and you add more and more to your plate. Instead of talking about doing that big thing for five years but not taking action, do the small thing now and in five years you may even be well ahead of what your big goal initially was.

25

Actions Towards Self-Care

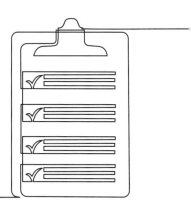

TO FOLLOW ON FROM THE PREVIOUS CHAPTER, YOU ARE going to start incorporating a few things each day to care for yourself. Start with one for your brain and mind, and one for your physical body because, as you have now gathered, what you do for your physical body has a direct implication on your brain health. Additionally, the simple act of doing something for yourself, while working on yourself, makes you feel better, increases your self-worth and also makes changing your narratives easier and easier.

This is all about turning what you have learnt into something you can now maintain moving forward. And because you are ever-evolving and always met with new experiences, some good and some bad, it is important to keep up your mental and emotional fitness. If you do the work, then recovering from heartbreak or disappointment or any emotional distress becomes more achievable and less daunting. Like someone who is agile and physically fit, when they have to go in for an operation, their rehabilitation journey is going to be a lot faster than someone who barely exercises or takes care of their body.

You don't have to prepare for the worst-case scenario in order to be able to overcome it; instead you are preparing yourself to be okay no matter what happens. The focus is on you and your relationship to yourself, and on being resilient. These are the things you can control. If you spend your life fearing the unknown, creating perfectionist ideals for your life and never wanting to take that next step until everything is perfect, then you will be at the mercy of external sources. You will always feel that you don't have the power and when you feel powerless you don't take action, you only react. It is up to you to make these changes and the changes start today.

EXERCISE

Activities to start doing daily

Meditate for ten or more minutes in the morning – this sets up your day in the calmest and happiest way. You reduce stress, lower your cortisol and get that healthy release of dopamine.

Avoid social media for the first hour of the day – social media will cause your dopamine to drop below baseline the longer you spend on it, making you less likely to feel primed and ready to start the day to dedicate your energy to the things that matter to you.

Get outside and move your body for at least twenty minutes in the sun and fresh air – this will increase your feel-good neurochemicals such as serotonin, dopamine and endorphins, which will relax you and lower your cortisol levels. Ideally do this first thing in the morning so you expose yourself to natural light, which is the healthiest way to wake up the brain and your circadian rhythm.

Journal every day and reflect on how things affected you and if or how you could rewrite the thoughts behind them – this is your opportunity to start rewriting how you approach things. It's the time of your day to record, rationalise and replace. You'll go to bed feeling like you have addressed anything that was on your mind and causing you angst if you put it on paper and out of your head, which will make it easier for you to wind down.

Feel free to add to this list as much as you like, but it shouldn't feel like a chore. It should feel like you are doing yourself a favour. If you feel like it is too much to start with, then pick your top two favourites and add another one to the list each week. This is something that will eventually become part of what you do and will no longer feel like an effort. Persistence and consistency are key in everything you do.

26

The Importance of Habits and Rituals for Self-Love

CREATING HABITS CAN BE ONE OF THE MOST REWARDING things you can do for yourself.

Habits or rituals are something that our brains love. The brain loves repetition because it allows us to form patterns and outsource tasks to our subconscious mind so we can perform them with less effort. We create habits whether we want to or not. The brain forms patterns around behaviours that serve a need, a want or a craving, and when we do it enough then we feel like we can't function properly without it. We all have them, the good and the bad. No matter how unorganised you are, you have created habits. These could be:

- your morning coffee
- how you shower
- how you drive
- needing to have something sweet before bed
- smoking
- meditating
- checking your phone regularly without even getting an alert.

It's essential to understand the importance of a habit and what it provides in your life in order for you to make new ones and override old ones.

EXERCISE

Ask yourself, where in my life right now have I created a habit that benefits me? And what habits do I have that don't benefit me? Am I really good at my skincare routine? Am I always on time? Do I meditate at the same time every day?

Do I have a habit of cancelling on people? Do I have a behavioural habit that is bad for my physical or mental health? Do I sleep in past my alarm every day and then feel rushed? Do I stay up so late on my phone or watching TV that I never truly wind down?

The first benefit of creating a habit is stability. It grounds us. Even the most adventurous person needs to feel grounded. Stability represents control and, more importantly, what YOU can control. When you feel you have autonomy and control over certain aspects of your life, you feel safer, more grounded and, ironically, more open to instability (otherwise known as adventure) in other areas of your life. If there was absolutely nothing that you had control over, if you had zero independence and no ability to make choices, or if everything in your life felt unstable, you would be in a constant state of stress, anxiety or depression, only able to react to everything coming your way. You would not be able to build up to something, as each day would be completely different. You wouldn't know how to rely on yourself. When this happens, people can become super controlling with their partner or a perfectionist with their work; they are scrambling to gain some sort of control in areas where they will never achieve it. When you provide control and a level of stability in your mind and in your life, you then have more room for spontaneity because you have security. You are then more likely to welcome the unknown, finding it exciting. You are more likely to feel stable and grounded enough that other things that occur outside of you won't affect you too heavily.

Habits and rituals allow you to form a sense of stability and control over your life and your actions; they are choices you make that become a subconscious habit. The more you do something, the better you get at it. And like I mentioned before, growth is one of the pillars of self-love. Once something becomes subconscious, you no longer need to think about it. You do it automatically and if you don't do it, you feel off. This here is the sweet spot. You now have freed up your conscious mind to do more creative things, be present for other tasks and be more efficient at work. Another benefit of having a habit is that you stop needing to make decisions around it, and it saves you a lot of time each morning and night, which adds up to a lot of mental effort that can be directed elsewhere.

We normally will put off doing something that is boring, uncomfortable or painful. And the longer we contemplate it, the more chances we have of backing out or abandoning the task all together. You give yourself too much time to side with the devil on your shoulder and then it's too late. A habit cuts out the decision-making process of doing a task. It is so embedded in you, almost like a ritual, that you just do it without deliberating and, because you do it daily, you save so much time as you get more and more efficient with it. Before you know it, you have knocked out a bunch of household tasks and exercises and the day has barely started, and you are feeling fresh in the mind as you have not used up your decision-making quota for the day. You are ready to put your mind to the things that really matter to you. When you do this for yourself, the way you feel about yourself begins to transform faster than you could have imagined. After three days you will notice a shift, and after just ten days you will feel completely different.

Now it's time to create your morning and evening routines. I'll lay out a few options or examples here, but before we start let's lay down some ground rules.

Limit distractions. When you are going through your daily habit or ritual, you want to do it in the same order every day (whenever possible) and, ideally, it should take roughly the same amount of time. If you open yourself up for phone calls, checking social media apps or whatever else, then you throw yourself off and you defeat the purpose of making this an easy, seamless routine.

To start with, try to limit your routine to one or two hours. Don't fill your day up, as the longer the list of things to do, the more likely you are to avoid it or put it off. I personally have a few different routines throughout the day, but my morning one is under half an hour.

The earlier the better. If you can set a morning routine, you have set the tone for the day. Don't wait until the night unless you have a damn good reason, for example, you work night shifts.

When you create a habit, it is like you are outsourcing a job to your subconscious mind. You no longer have to contemplate or put in excessive effort. You don't have to decide anything. It is done. The effort of your conscious mind is no longer needed and it can be put to use somewhere else.

Once we reach the limit of our decision-making quota, we feel flat. We can't choose an outfit, what to eat, what movie to watch; we are indecisive and unenthusiastic. The problem is when this indecisiveness starts earlier and earlier in the day, on important things like discussions, career decisions, studying or writing an essay. If you eat into this valuable decision-making quota, then you struggle later in the day. Routines are the answer. Why do certain CEOs always wear the same outfit? It's one less decision. I can guarantee that most of the successful people you know have a routine in place that helps streamline their day.

With no routine, you become more indecisive, and with indecision comes stress. The more stressed you are, the harder it is to focus, remember something, hone your creativity or get into a flow state. Something as basic and mundane as having a routine is one of the keys to feeling happy, feeling great about yourself and increasing your self-love.

EXERCISE

Morning and evening routines

From today, I want you to write down a new routine for your mornings and evenings. Start small and basic. Maybe just the first and last fifteen minutes of the day.

Here is an example of a morning routine:

- Wake up
- Drink half a litre of water
- Brush teeth
- Make bed
- Meditate for ten minutes
- Get dressed.

In the mornings, try to do each task in the same order with no time wasted in between. You are in the zone and it is like a ritual for yourself.

Ideally, during your routine, you want to make it all about you. Your phone should be on silent and away from your line of sight. No calls, emails, texts, social media, NOTHING. Try to stay off the phone for the first thirty minutes. I do for the first hour unless I need to call someone to meet for a workout or walk.

Then the evening can look something like this:

- Brush teeth
- Shower
- Do skincare routine
- Take vitamins
- Journal for five to ten minutes
- Meditate for five minutes
- Read or listen to a story for twenty to thirty minutes
- Sleep!

Again, you want to have minimal stimulation before going to bed. Try to brush your teeth at least forty-five minutes before sleep, as the bathroom light is normally very bright and sends signals to your brain to stay awake. The strong minty taste of toothpaste doesn't help in reducing stimulation either. Don't fall asleep scrolling through your phone. Finish that before your bedtime routine starts. Your wind-down will be better and you will start to feel better about yourself when you prioritise your own peace of mind first and last thing in the day. You will feel calmer and less anxious and you will wake up a lot happier. It sounds so basic, but routines allow the brain to create peace. Peace allows for less stress and better connectivity, which makes for a calmer, happier brain.

Plan your routines TODAY and do them for two weeks straight. I can guarantee you if you do them without fail, after the two weeks you won't be able to live without them. Of course, you don't have to follow my routine. Make it your own, but make it simple, repeatable, enjoyable and not too long.

27

Finding Wins
in the Process

I THINK IT IS IMPORTANT TO HAVE A VISION FOR YOUR FUTURE, whether it be a one- or five-year vision. It's good to set goals and targets and get pumped for them. Targets are great and super helpful to make up part of what motivates you, but it's important that they are not the only part.

When you look at what makes up a lifestyle change, you want to implement things in your life that are sustainable, that can become part of the new you. If you are only doing something for the end result, then you are likely not enjoying the process; you are telling yourself it is temporary and, when (and if) that goal is achieved, you then revert to your old ways. You never truly changed. Your drivers – the things that make you tick – didn't change. So, if you want to create lasting change, if you want to level up and raise your standards in your life, the change you implement should be permanent, lasting, sustainable and, hopefully, enjoyable.

Now this is where I like to split things up into two goal categories: lifestyle goals and milestone goals. Milestone goals are the things that you only have to achieve once, like rehabbing an injury, getting a degree, travelling to the other side of the world – that kind of stuff. You build up to this event and once it is done, it is done. Then we have lifestyle goals. This is stuff like feeling healthy, working out, weight loss (yes, this is lifestyle and not milestone), speaking another language, your career, a sport you play.

I think that people too often place lifestyle goals into the milestone category and by doing so they make the goal a temporary thing and don't consider it part of their life in the long term. When I did my degree, I understood it was a once-off and my final semester, while extremely time-consuming, was doable because it was not a long-term thing. There was a goal in sight and it was a good motivator for me to work towards. I was able to stick it out because I knew I wouldn't have to sustain that crazy lifestyle forever. If you do that with a goal such as weight loss, what will you do once you have achieved that goal? This is the problem with crash diets. If the diet doesn't serve your lifestyle, then it won't work in the long term. If you are suffering every day counting down the days for it to be over, how sustainable do you think the results will be?

Setting the wrong kind of goals can have an impact on your beliefs about yourself and your abilities. You take a step back and feel bad because you didn't achieve the goal when, in reality, you were not the problem, your goal structure was.

THE NEUROSCIENCE OF SELF-LOVE

EXERCISE

Write all your goals down how you normally would word them and split your goals up into the two categories of milestone and lifestyle goals. Do they belong in these categories? Which goals should be moved to the lifestyle category? Next to each goal in the lifestyle category, write down ways you can integrate it into your life and make it long term, without it being a punishment for you.

It's crucial that you start to find joy in the doing, in the taking action, regardless of the final outcome.

Let's look at exercise for example. If you only exercise to lose weight and achieve a certain ideal image in your head, then, when you achieve that image, would you stop exercising? Or what if you never achieve that image? Would you stop exercising? What if you found reasons to do what you do that are not tied to the final outcome?

Every time I would try to tackle an essay for my least favourite subject I would drag my feet to the desk, procrastinate, complain the whole way through to anyone who would listen and, once done, complain about how hard it was. Then I started to change my tune a bit and although it didn't make me LOVE statistics, I started to enjoy the process.

I started saying to myself, right, how much writing can I do in thirty minutes? Who cares if it's not perfect; let's see if I can set a record. My focus then went on competing with my last word count record, so I stopped avoiding the task or talking about how bad it was. It wasn't THAT bad. I was lucky to be doing a degree that I loved overall, I just needed to get out of that mental slump.

Although not everything I wrote in those thirty minutes was useful, maybe half of it was, and that half was more than I used to get done in two hours. It's amazing how much more productive you can be when you shift the focus to enjoy the process. In my final year of uni (the year I started implementing this technique) I always handed assignments in at least three days before the due date. I just got it done, regardless of how much I loved the subject, because it was about the process and it was a challenge and I liked feeling like I was capable.

When you change your focus from being purely on the end result to what you are capable of achieving each day, you will start to enjoy the daily efforts. They become what excites you for the next day. And when you reach that point, you become unstoppable. You no longer expect your happiness to come at the end. You get it now. That is where lasting change happens.

Make something part of you, part of your lifestyle and find joy in the doing. Here are some examples of things you may find boring or too much of an effort and how to change your mentality around them:

- I hate working out – I love that I can push through feeling out of breath. I love the rests I get after that effort. I love that I never notice how good breathing feels except for this moment when I catch my breath.
- I hate catching the bus to work – I love that this is my opportunity each day to read or listen to a book. It's my time and I don't have to answer to anyone in this moment.
- I hate cleaning the house – This is one of the times I can blast the music and get in the zone, while getting shit done at the same time. I feel pumped afterwards.
- I hate waking up early – I love that feeling, knowing that I have the power to control my own actions by getting out of bed. It means I can control a lot more than I give myself credit for.

For everything you complain about or put off doing, find something great to associate it with like in all the previous examples. Just like a conditioned response, you eventually condition yourself to anticipate the good association with each task. Your focus shifts to a completely different place. If you are saying, 'I don't have anything I can associate this with', then find something. There is always something. It is your willingness to find something that makes you capable of enjoying it.

See what your work represents. Hard work represents a lot about who you are, your character. Learning can be enjoyable if you don't put so much pressure on yourself. Instead of thinking, I need to get this degree over and done with, think, What awesome thing can I learn today and how can I apply it? Is it something I can teach someone else? I started doing that and, through my love of learning and sharing what I learnt, it led to me starting a podcast and a career I had never even imagined was possible for me. Chase the feeling, not the end result.

28

Improve Your Decision-Making Skills to Increase Your Confidence

HOW DO STRONG DECISION-MAKING SKILLS CONNECT TO self-love? When you learn to make decisions with determination, you learn to trust yourself. You get better at listening to your instincts and you start placing value on your choices. You listen to your wants more than your doubts. This builds confidence within yourself, you waste less time questioning yourself and spend more time focusing on your new decision and it feels good. When you feel good about yourself, your self-love expands. You also stop allowing your fear pathways to override your decisions. If you overthink something, neurochemicals like cortisol will strengthen these fear pathways and make it harder for your brain areas to communicate to arrive at logical conclusions.

Harvard psychologist Dan Gilbert shares in his many studies around decision-making that, in general, people are pretty horrible at estimating the outcome of something that will happen to them. This is different to a calculated bet. We are talking more about subjective experiences here. People in general make errors in predicting the odds of them gaining something out of a situation and they make errors in the value of what they would gain when it comes to experiences and life decisions. Calculating odds with what you are going to experience is different to calculating odds in rolling a die.

Another problem that we create for ourselves when it comes to making decisions about our life or future is that we compare things too much and that changes our perspective.

We compare things to the past instead of comparing things with the possible. Instead, we should be considering things as an isolated opportunity and whether it has value independent of external factors.

Gilbert also demonstrated another interesting point about decision-making. In a study where participants were asked to choose a photograph to keep, people who had the opportunity to make their decisions reversible were more unhappy with their final choice. And those who had to make an irreversible decision were not only happier with their decision but also were happier than they predicted they would be. Why is this? The group with the reversible decision got too caught up in the back and forth, the comparisons, in the 'what ifs', imagining what it could be like having the alternative option, so much so that they began to feel dissatisfied with their choice. The irreversible group knew they couldn't change their mind, so stopped contemplating the past, they then put their focus on appreciating their choice and ended up loving it more than they thought they would.

If you think that you cannot live without something or someone, you will always be scared to make a big change and this will keep you in a place of limbo. You keep comparing the unknown future to your current reality and making conclusions. If you have one foot in the future and one foot in the past, you will be stuck between the two and you won't enjoy either option. You will have a fear of missing out and a fear of losing your old life.

As if that is not enough, you can also add self-doubt to that list. When you start to doubt your ability to choose the right path, job, outfit, person, home or anything else in your life, you get stuck in a vicious cycle of not trusting your ability to make a decision or to stick with it and, because of this, you become more indecisive at the next opportunity and then you are dissatisfied with your choice.

Now, how do we flip this around? Simple. You just make one call and stick to it. When you commit to something and you make your decision irreversible, you become more satisfied and, in most cases, HAPPIER than you expected yourself to be some time after the decision is made, because you stop making comparisons with what is no longer available.

What if the decision was the wrong one?

You can only ever truly know if a decision is wrong by giving it a go and getting it out of your system. Even in this scenario, you STILL never have to think about it because that choice, that option you took has now been discarded. You have turned that irreversible decision into something useful. You know it didn't work out for you, it may have led you to something new, or maybe it wasn't what you thought it was going to be, so you never have to think about it again. This is actually a good outcome. Think about the alternative!

Most people would talk themselves out of doing something because it may be the 'wrong' idea. But in most cases in life you SAVE time even if the decision was wrong, because you chose it, you committed, you experienced what there was to experience, eliminated it and you moved on. All the while, everyone around you is still stuck on the two options they had and not done anything about it out of fear of it not working out. You are now onto the next thing, and the next thing, while also growing and nurturing your creativity and resilience, creating new networks and ideas so you can be more equipped for the next experience. When something doesn't work out, it just provides you with more experience and more proximity to where you want to be because you have greater clarity. You also gained a skill or a lesson along the way.

Okay great, now that we have established that, how do you go about making a decision irreversible? There are a few things. Firstly, you can limit your time to make that decision. Take choosing a movie to watch, for example. The longer you take to decide, the more irritable and less present you are going to be if you spent an hour deciding on the film. If you only had three options or three minutes to decide, you would be more present and more definitive with your decision. So create time limits for smaller decisions such as outfits, online purchases, movies to watch or items on a menu. Literally, set yourself a time limit of a few minutes and, once that limit is over, that decision cannot be reversed! You will notice that you will start making decisions faster and be happier with the decision you have made.

With big decisions, such as changing careers, moving homes, cities or countries, leaving a toxic relationship or making a big financial purchase, you want to start investing in the decision that you want the most. Not the conservative one, not the one everyone has told you to make. The one that speaks to you more. Of course, these decisions have to be calculated: can you financially afford it, do you have the skills and so on.

What are some things you can think of for big decisions? Some examples could be:

- buying the plane ticket before you have planned any part of the move (my personal favourite – I did this when I went to France)
- signing up for a course
- actively applying for jobs and physically going to interviews instead of just looking at what jobs are available
- deleting your toxic ex's number and all the old messages.

EXERCISE

Write down a few of your own examples that are relevant to your life situation.

What are some things you can do this week to put things into motion? What actions can you take to make your decisions more definite? Could you give yourself a time limit or reduce the number of options to make it easier to narrow down your decision?

29

Reach Your Point of No Return

YOU HAVE REACHED THE END OF THIS BOOK AND, HOPEFULLY, the start of your journey to the new and improved 2.0 version of you. As you put into practice everything you have learnt here, I want you to also say goodbye to your old self. A true detachment from your old patterns needs to happen so you can embrace everything new you have going for you. If you are in between both versions of yourself, you will likely revert to your old self, and your old patterns, behaviours and thoughts. Now is the time to make some irreversible decisions about who you are going to be and raise your standards for what you now deem to be acceptable for you moving forward. It's time to reinvent yourself.

EXERCISE

To begin, I want you to write down all the things you have been doing intentionally or unintentionally that you want to let go of. Write it all down. Narratives you tell yourself, your internal working model, things you use to pacify yourself, habits that you get into that prevent you from taking action on the things that matter most to you.

Then below all of this, write down not only WHAT will change but also why you want it to change and how you will implement those changes for yourself. Write down why it is so important to you that you raise your standards for what is acceptable. Because it comes down to you. No one else is going to come along and change how you think, and it's not going to change by itself. Only your experiences and efforts can do that for you. This decision is empowering and it's the start of your journey to true self-love and to maintaining that level of self-love throughout your life.

Once you have written all this down, fold the paper up and save it in a safe location, then set yourself a reminder one year from today to open that letter and look back to see what you have been able to change for yourself. Nothing drastic has to happen, no big event, just the small actions in this book (and anything else you choose to add on top).

Knowing that that piece of paper is there will serve as a driver for you. Each morning when you wake up, imagine yourself reading that paper and seeing how much has changed for yourself. Every time you are about to procrastinate on something that is important to you, think about that paper and ask yourself, 'If I don't do this small action, what will this mean for my future self?'

Always be working on yourself; you are ever-evolving so don't just stop here. Stay curious, pay attention to yourself, learn from your mistakes and experiences, relish them!

THE NEUROSCIENCE OF SELF-LOVE

Keep moving forward and always be willing to grow, evolve and adapt. Action is always going to feel better than inaction. So just start, and keep that ball rolling no matter how small each step is.

I hope that this book has given you a better insight into yourself, your brain, why you think the way you do and why you do the things you do. My hope is that you now feel more empowered and that you feel like you have the tools to make some changes to get to a place of true self-love. As you have noticed, it's all internal and nothing to do with the external. It's all about you.

It's time to reinvent yourself. And you can reinvent yourself many, many times over. Don't second-guess, act now, and that reset button is there for you whenever you need it.

And lastly, remember to be kind to yourself, be kind to your brain. Don't take shit from anyone and especially don't take shit from yourself.

Danke!

Acknowledgements

This book would not have been possible if it were not for all the researchers and scientists who have come before me who share a passion and curiosity for neuroscience, and who have made all this fascinating information available.

I would also like to thank my abuela Lidia, who taught me resilience and how to take things in your stride; my abuelita Mireya, who taught me how to always see the best in everyone, and to find fun in every moment; my abuelo Jose, who taught me dedication and the importance of working for something; and my abuelo Clemente, who taught me perseverance, devotion and appreciation.

I want to thank my parents for their amazing love, and for teaching me to be hungry for knowledge; my sister Stefanie, as she is the person I look up to the most in this world; and my partner, Tyrone, for being such a light in my life.

To my amazing family and best friends, thank you for giving me the best relationships I could imagine.

And to all my beans (my podcast listeners), you guys are incredible. Thank you for sharing what I do, and for your unwavering love and support. It never goes unnoticed, and I am grateful every day.